why hello there...

inspired

[IN-SPY-ERED]

Adjective

DEFINITION

1. To lead by example and fill women with an inspired spirit.

2. To produce a deep desire for wanting MORE out of life.

3. To live an inspirational existence.

4. To influence positive change.

To fill myself and others with the urge or ability to do or feel something, especially to do something creative. It's that fluttering feeling in your chest. That sudden surge of electricity coursing through your body. The quickening of the heart.

Feeling INSPIRED is moving.

– WHAT TO EXPECT –

01 INTRODUCTION

02 START BELIEVING

03 DREAM BIG

04 BEAUTY

05 NOURISH

06 NOW MOVE IT

- WHAT TO EXPECT -

Why Inspired? LORNA'S Story

INSPIRED is a word we use obsessively at Lorna Jane and I think it's because it best describes what we do as a brand, as well as 'WHY' we love what we do and why we are excited to do it every day.

If I'm being completely honest, I only started designing activewear because I wanted to INSPIRE myself and other women in my life to be more active. And I started talking about my Active Living philosophy because I wanted to INSPIRE you to Move Nourish and Believe in yourself, so you could feel as motivated and energised as I do every single day!

I guess I always knew I had something to share with the world and it turned out that Lorna Jane, Active Living and Move Nourish Believe were it!

I have been visualising (and mood boarding) this book with my team for a while now, and the main reason I wanted it to be about inspiration was because of our customers. Each time I met and spoke with supporters of our brand, 9 times out of 10 they'd tell me, the reason they loved Lorna Jane, me, my team and Move Nourish Believe was because we INSPIRED them!

INSPIRED them to be fit.

INSPIRED them to be healthy.

INSPIRED them to Believe in themselves.

We ultimately INSPIRED them to get more out of their lives by giving more of themselves every single day through Active Living!

I think everyone deserves to live an inspired life and at Lorna Jane we exist for just that. To INSPIRE our customers and encourage them to learn, grow and improve every day.

□□□

I BELIEVE TO BE INSPIRATIONAL YOU NEED TO LIVE AN INSPIRED LIFE

And INSPIRED was created to give you all the knowledge and insights we have collected over the years in anticipation of this very day. The day you would find it and the day your journey of inspiration would begin!

Because we want to inspire YOU!

I decided to create this INSPIRED project with Ash and our team at MNB because they embody all things inspiration and positivity. So it absolutely made sense to me that they come on board and we work on this project together.

Ash heads up my MNB team and has been trailblazing Move Nourish Believe globally since I handed it over to her in the early days as a simple blog. It was a tough decision for me and finding the right person took time and careful consideration. But it turns out she has been the perfect fit and it has flourished into a full-blown website, with an engaged global community and a team of inspiring women that have taken my daily practice and infused it into the hearts and minds of so many women all over the world.

INSPIRED is our biggest project to date and our mission is to create a movement of inspiration all over the world. It's a coffee table book because we want it to sit centre stage in your life, be on-hand 24/7 and not on a bookshelf somewhere in your house where you could easily forget about it. We want it to be so beautiful that you can flip the cover either way and it will still look amazing on display in your home. We want it to be your go-to reference to get INSPIRED about life and all of the joys it has to offer.

But this book will only INSPIRE you if you let it! So what are you waiting for? It's time to lose yourself in the beautiful imagery and captivating content as you become a little more INSPIRED every time you turn the page.

MNB

Lana Jane x

Our leading lady LORNA JANE CLARKSON
with MNB editor ASHLEIGH HIPWOOD

OUR PROMIS
ROMISE OUR
UR PROMISE
MISE OUR P
UR PROMISE
MISE OUR P
OUR PROMIS
ROMISE OUR

Our promise to you...

We promise to **INSPIRE** you every single day.

This promise will not falter, fizzle or dim.

Why?

Because you are the **reason** we **exist**.

The very reason WHY we do what we do is to **inspire** you
to live your best life through Active Living.

That's what you **deserve**.

We believe that life should never be short of inspiration,
so we **PROMISE** to **CREATE**.

Create images, WORDS and activewear so BEAUTIFUL, they
INSPIRE you to wake up with **purpose** and **passion**.

We promise to be **AUTHENTIC**, speak from the **heart** and uncover
new and exciting ways to embrace Active Living.

It is our promise to give you **MORE**.

More of what you love. More of what you need.

Inspiration knows no bounds.

And we **will never stop**. INSPIRING. you.

HOW TO SET A MOVE NOURISH BELIEVE INTENTION

Before you bury your head in this book, know this...

There's one very important ritual we practise every day, one, which we believe, keeps our inspired spirit alive and gives us a daily purpose.

It's a little something we like to call setting an MNB Intention. A daily commitment to living your best, active life through Move Nourish Believe.

The way it works is quite simple really. Commit to your daily Move Nourish Believe goals and you will be a step closer to where you really want to be. There simply is no better way to stay focused, driven and on purpose.

M: I will get up and move my body every morning

N: I will have something green with every meal

B: I will create an inspired life

M: Go do yoga... and actually go

N: Experiment with fermented foods

B: Cherish precious moments with my family and friends

t

in

happy girls are
the most
inspiring

Believe

It's probably one of the most commonly
used words in the hallways of Lorna Jane,
and with very good reason.

Believe has the power to change lives and we know without a
shadow of a doubt that believing in yourself and what you can
achieve is imperative to move forward in life.

You cannot live a positive life with a negative mind...
nor can you achieve those big reach-for-the-stars goals if you
don't believe you can catch them first!

So no matter where you want to go or what you want to
achieve in life, the best thing you can do to make those big,
beautiful dreams a reality is first and foremost, believe.

Because everything starts with believe.

ロJロ

HAVE A
VISION

If our leading lady Lorna Jane Clarkson has taught us anything, it's that seeing is believing! And the first thing you see upon walking through the doors of LJ HQ are vision boards, each adorned with a collation of beautiful images and motivational mantras. Having a vision is what living an INSPIRED life is all about!

HOW TO MAKE A VISION BOARD

Vision boards are one of the most valuable tools you can have to help manifest your deepest dreams and desires, plus they're super fun and easy to make. Vision Boards (also known as mood or dream boards) are perfect for setting all sorts of goals from fitness and health-related intentions right through to career or even finances.

1. Collate a series of inspiring and empowering pictures, quotes, words, photographs, affirmations, magazine clippings or even possessions that represent or reflect what you're trying to manifest.

2. Get crafty and creative and arrange them beautifully on a cork or pin board, remembering to keep it clean, simple and focused on one theme or topic to stop attracting clutter into your life.

3. Position it in an open place that's likely to catch your eye frequently like your bedside table or even your desk at work so you're constantly reminded of that overarching goal.

ALWAYS REMEMBER...

1. BE CLEAR ON WHAT YOU'RE TRYING TO MANIFEST
Don't put mixed messages out into the universe; it will only attract mess into your life.

2. BELIEVE TO ACHIEVE
When you combine the power of positivity with the power of visualisation, you're setting yourself up to win!

3. LOOK'N'LEARN
Look at your vision board regularly to remind yourself what you're trying to manifest.

THE POWER OF POSITIVITY

NEVER UNDERESTIMATE THE POWER OF POSITIVITY.

A positive attitude is one of the most valuable things you can have in life. It has the ability to turn even the worst day into a wonderful one, but perhaps the best thing about positivity is that it's a completely infectious quality that EVERYBODY can have... and radiate!

Think of those happy shiny people in your life. You know the ones, who always manage to exude so much joy and optimism that just being in their presence gives you an instant hit of happy? It's no coincidence

they always have something to smile about; it's the basic law of attraction. Positive people generate positive thoughts and positive thoughts breed positive results.

It's one of those things that the more you give, the more you get... so always keep those happy vibes high and alive.

While it's easy to be a glass half full kinda girl when life is blue skies and butterflies, it's important to keep projecting this attitude when the clouds start to roll in. Why? Because just one thought of something happy is powerful enough to release endorphins, those feel good chemicals in the brain that can turn a scowl into a smile in a matter of moments.

When you make the decision to be positive and train your brain to see the good in every situation you'll soon start to notice just how much good there is in this world.

So if you're in the market for a positive life, you can totally Make It Happen, it all starts with a positive mind.

how to be a
BELIEVER

OUR BELIEVE LIST:

1. COUNT YOUR BLESSINGS, <u>EVERY</u> SINGLE ONE OF THEM
2. MAKE TIME FOR MEDITATION
3. ADOPT A YOGA PRACTICE
4. ALWAYS HAVE A DREAM IN YOUR SIGHTS
5. MAKE <u>MINDFULNESS</u> AN AM TO PM THING
6. SURROUND YOURSELF WITH POSITIVE PEOPLE
7. BE YOUR OWN BIGGEST FAN
8. PRACTICE GRATITUDE DAILY
9. LIVE IN THE MOMENT AND <u>ALWAYS</u> BE PRESENT
10. SAY [THANK YOU] MORE
11. GIVE COMPLIMENTS DAILY
12. TELL YOUR FAMILY HOW MUCH YOU LOVE THEM
13. DONATE YOUR TIME TO SOMEONE IN NEED
14. DO THINGS THAT MAKE YOUR HEART SING.

WE ALL NEED TO _LIVE_ MORE. WE ALL NEED TO BREATHE DEEPLY.
WE ALL NEED TO GET OUT OF OUR HEADS. WE ALL NEED TO _STOP_ WORRYING.
WE ALL NEED TO FORGET OUR FEARS, AND WE ALL NEED TO REMEMBER
WHAT TRULY MATTERS...

PRACTISE MINDFULNESS

WE'VE ALL EXPERIENCED THOSE MOMENTS OF SUBCONSCIOUSLY 'DOING,' AND NOT 'BEING.'

You know, when life is going at 100-miles-an-hour and we kick into autopilot, going about everyday tasks mindlessly? Life is a beautiful gift and every day is filled with magical moments, and every second of it deserves to be wholeheartedly lived.

So are we really living it? Are we really appreciating every moment? Savouring every bite? Feeling everything deeply?

INSPIRATION calls for a little perspective. To be creative, to grow, to prosper and flourish, being present is an essential component. The concept of mindfulness is about being present in the moment, and being conscious of making the most out of each and every day. It's about appreciating the little things (those actions in everyday life that you consciously do, but sub-consciously ignore) and not letting life pass you by.

Mindfulness will help you feel the cool breeze on your skin, put down your phone, engage in meaningful conversations and gaze up at the stars. Active Living is living every minute, every second with purpose and intent. To be INSPIRED you need to live a meaningful existence. Mindfulness is the key to unlocking that deep, inspired human within us all.

SOS

DO YOU HAVE ONE?

A Sister of Support is something we MNB Girls affectionately refer to as a SOS and the role she plays in our life is even more valuable to our wellbeing than a sports bra or cold-pressed juicer.

A **SOS** is an around-the-clock kind of friend. No matter the issue, a SOS is positive and relentless in finding a solution.

A **SOS** offers maximum support at any time of the day or night, it's perfectly acceptable to receive a text message at 5.30am reminding you not to hit snooze for the seventh time and get your butt to boot camp!

A **SOS** doesn't need a cue to 'be there' she intuitively knows and shows up exactly when you need her with a block of dark chocolate and box of tissues in tow.

A **SOS** leads by example knowing all too well that her positive actions will influence others.

A **SOS** is inspirational. She's got your back at all times and pushes you harder than anybody else because she believes in you.

A **SOS** motivates you like no other. Sometimes you wonder if she was a motivational speaker in a past life.

A **SOS** will help you find a way to get your sparkle back when you feel as though your light is beginning to dim.

Life is better when you have a Sister of Support. And we know because we have experienced first hand the sheer magic that comes from having a friend who without even knowing it, inspires you every single day.

TRUTHBOMB:

SURROUND YOURSELF WITH THE ONES WHO HELP YOU REALISE YOUR TRUE POTENTIAL, EVEN WHEN YOU MAY NOT SEE IT YOURSELF.

SISTER OF SUPPORT (SOS)

(N.) A WOMAN, FRIEND, GIRL OR ACTUAL SISTER WHO IS YOUR SUPPORT SYSTEM FOR ALL THINGS ACTIVE LIVING. SHE HAS YOUR BACK EVERY STEP OF THE WAY TO HELP YOU LIVE YOUR BEST LIFE.

Synonyms: life coach, personal trainer, chef, shopping buddy, real talker, motivational speaker, inspiration, 5km walk & talk partner, weight spotter, advice giver, best friend.

WHO'S SOS ARE YOU?

[A]

Believe

REMINDER
''''''''''''''''''''
OOO

RIGHT NOW

In this moment,
I CHOOSE TO breathe
TO STOP, BE MINDFUL,
& COUNT MY
blessings.

For no matter what,
I will NOT give up on
WHAT I WANT MOST
for what
I want now.

I will let the
POWER OF POSITIVITY reign
supreme
in all my thoughts.

& I PROMISE that right now,
tomorrow & the next day, I will
make my dreams BIGGER than my doubts.

I CHOOSE to BELIEVE!

DREAM

AND BIGGER AND BIGGER AND BIGGER...

For a decent dose of 'life advice' there is one acronym we always turn to…

WHAT WOULD LORNA DO?

LORNA C...

*What Would Lorna Do?
That million-dollar question we ask
ourselves in any given situation.
We take 5 with our leading lady
Lorna Jane Clarkson to get the
lowdown on dreaming BIG
and how to achieve both
happiness and success in life.*

DREAM BIG

Dare to dream because the future
belongs to those who believe in the
beauty of their dreams; and actually find
the courage and determination to follow
through and pursue them.

LIVE WITH PASSION

Find a career that you can wake up to
every day and be passionate about. A
career that involves doing things that
you would choose to do even if you
weren't getting paid for it.

BE COURAGEOUS

Find the courage to write your own story and live an authentic life. The courage to be yourself, the courage to make change when it's needed, the courage to stand up for what you believe in and the courage to make the hard decisions in life.

MINDSET IS EVERYTHING

Never sit back, relax and become lazy... instead have the mindset to improve what you're doing every day.

MAKE AN IMPRESSION

It's never a good idea to sit on the sidelines of your own life. So if you want to move forward; take up space, have an opinion and absolutely go out and follow your dreams with gusto!

KEEP CHANGING

We live in a fast-paced world and you can never assume that just because you did it one way today, you can do it the same way next time. Keep moving, keep changing and never be predictable.

ACCEPT THAT IT'S GOING TO BE HARD

Learn to get comfortable with that feeling of being uncomfortable.

TAKE RISKS & NEVER NEVER NEVER GIVE UP

Don't quit on what you really want to do. I believe without a doubt, that the person with the big dreams is so much more powerful than the one with all the facts! And more often than not, you can bet that the moment you're ready to quit on your dream is usually the moment right before the miracle happens.

33

THE
DREAM
IS
FREE

THE CHASE IS SOLD SEPARATELY

Hey there earlybird!
In our eyes, the way you spend your morning is
ultimately the way you'll spend the rest of your day…
so make it an inspiring one! WE'VE GOT SIX
REASONS why getting up with the sun can make
you more successful!

1. THERE ARE LESS DISTRACTIONS IN THE MORNING

We know how crazy life can get, so crossing a few things off your to-do list whilst everyone is sleeping puts you one step ahead of the game and absolutely on the road to success.

2. MORE TIME TO 'MOVE-IT'

Morning people are wmore successful at motivating themselves to exercise on a regular basis. So knock it off first thing in the morning and start the day ready to take on the world.

3. YOU WILL HAVE TIME FOR BREAKFAST

Getting up early gives you more time to prepare and enjoy a nutritious breakfast. Eating well in the morning sets the tone for the rest of your day and we all know that when we fuel our bodies correctly it won't let us down!

4. YOU'LL BE MORE PRODUCTIVE

Waking up early gives you more hours in the day to do the things that you love and the things that inspire you, which puts you in a productive frame of mind for the rest of the day. The later you wake up, the more likely you are to feel stressed as you rush around trying to get everything done.

5. YOU'LL BE HAPPIER

Research shows that morning people tend to be happier and healthier, and we think it's because they get so much done at the start of the day that they have more time later to do the things that they love.

6. SUCCESSFUL PEOPLE ARE ALREADY DOING IT

Look around… it's the successful people in your neighbourhood that you'll see running on the treadmill at 5am or picking up their green smoothie bright and early on the way to work. They have taken advantage of that extra hour in the morning and are using it to get more out of their life.

So what are you waiting for? BE ONE OF THEM!

"Up early… got dreams to chase"

RISE & SHINE

10 THINGS
LORNA JANE GIRLS HAVE IN COMMON

1. THEY *ALWAYS* BACK THEIR DREAMS AND IDEAS, NO MATTER HOW SILLY THEY MAY SEEM TO OTHERS

2. THEY DON'T DREAM ABOUT SUCCESS, THEY WAKE UP AND *WORK HARD FOR IT*

3. THEY NEVER SHY AWAY FROM A CHALLENGE AND AREN'T AFRAID TO TAKE RISKS

4. THEY LIVE HONESTLY AND AUTHENTICALLY AND ARE NOT AFRAID TO BE 100% EXACTLY WHO THEY ARE

5. THEY ARE CONFIDENT IN THEMSELVES & *BELIEVE* IN THEIR OWN TALENT AND ABILITY

6. THEY AREN'T AFRAID TO ROLL UP THEIR SLEEVES AND GET THEIR HANDS *A LITTLE DIRTY*

7. THEY ARE PASSIONATE AND GO ABOUT EVERYTHING THEY *DO WITH ENTHUSIASM*

8. THEY DON'T WAIT FOR OPPORTUNITIES, THEY GO OUT AND *CREATE THEIR OWN*

9. THEY TREAT THEIR *BODY RIGHT* BECAUSE THEY KNOW IT WILL HELP THEM FEEL AND PERFORM AT THEIR BEST

10. THEY EMPOWER OTHER WOMEN INSTEAD OF BRINGING THEM DOWN

STRONG

VISIONARY

OUTSIDE THE BOX

CONFIDENCE

DRIVEN

Fearless

DOERS

YES

think SIDEWAYS

Determined

EXERCISE DAILY

FOCUS

Make it Happen

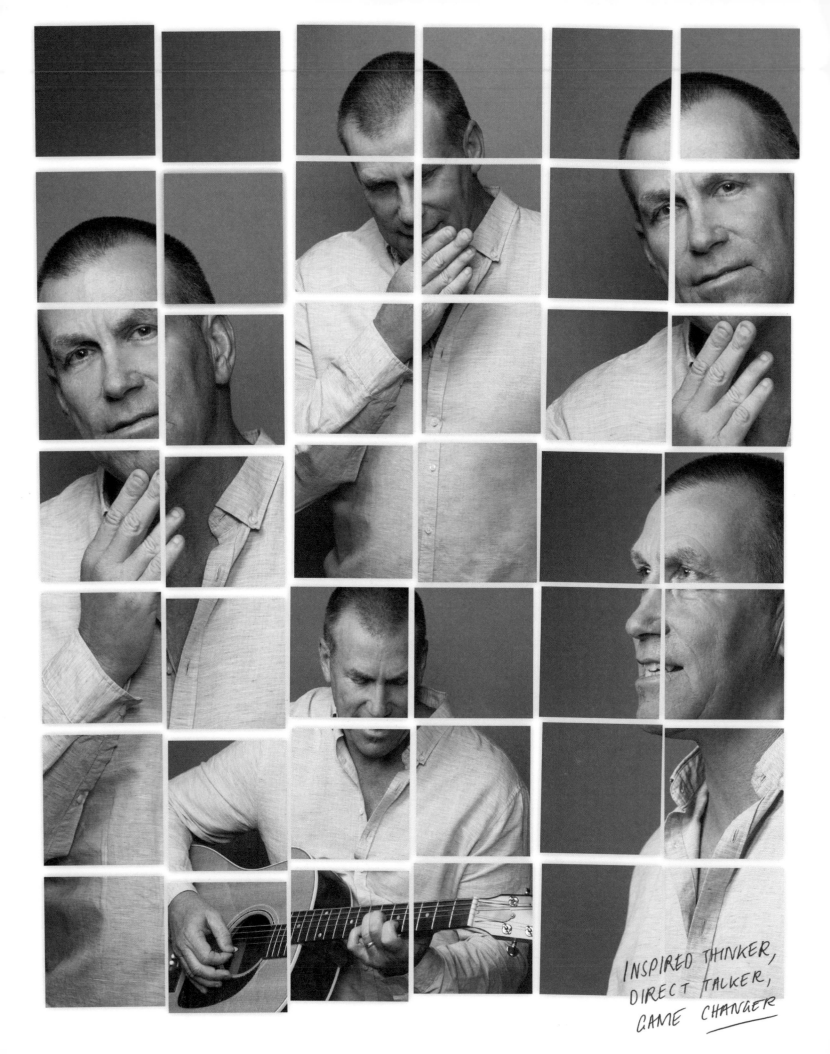

INSPIRED THINKER,
DIRECT TALKER,
GAME CHANGER

NAME BILL CLARKSON

OCCUPATION CEO

CURRENTLY INSPIRED BY... THE OPPORTUNITY OF ACTIVE LIVING & THE DAILY PRACTICE OF MNB.

WHY DO YOU DO WHAT YOU DO?

BECAUSE I LOVE WHAT I DO

WHAT OR WHO INSPIRES YOU MOST? PEOPLE WHO UNDERSTAND LIFE IS A JOURNEY & IT TAKES ALL TYPES TO HELP YOU UNDERSTAND GOOD + BAD / RIGHT + WRONG.

THE SECRET TO LIVING AN INSPIRED LIFE IS...

BELIEVE IN YOURSELF. YOU HAVE THE POWER!

WHAT GETS YOU OUT OF BED IN THE MORNING?

THE 5:00 AM ALARM CLOCK

THREE WORDS TO DESCRIBE YOURSELF

1. DETERMINED
2. FOCUSED
3. MISUNDERSTOOD

MY MEDITATION

FAVOURITE PLACE TO THINK?

MY GARDEN

WHAT IS HAPPINESS? FOR ME, IT IS A JOURNEY NOT A DESTINATION. I DON'T BELIEVE DOING THE SAME THING THROUGH LIFE MAKES YOU HAPPY, SO IT IS VERY MUCH ABOUT THE EXPERIENCE OF LIFE

IF YOU COULD HAVE ONE SUPERPOWER, WHAT WOULD IT BE?

THE ABILITY TO CHANGE HOW PEOPLE THINK.

IF YOU HAD TO BURY 3 THINGS IN A TIME CAPSULE FOR PEOPLE IN THE FUTURE – SAY 10,000 YEARS FROM NOW – WHAT WOULD YOU CHOOSE TO BURY?

MAYBE 3 CHOCOLATES - THERE IS NO POINT NOT GIVING THE OPENER OF THE CAPSULE A REASON TO SMILE.

WORKING WITH MY WIFE (LORNA JANE CLARKSON) IS...

THE BEST THING THAT COULD HAVE HAPPENED.

MAYBE MORE MEN SHOULD WORK WITH THEIR WIVES?

IT ISN'T THAT HARD IF YOU WANT THE SAME THINGS.

PICK A SIDE

ROLLING STONES OR ~~BEATLES~~?

EGGS. ~~POACHED~~ OR SCRAMBLED?

CHIPS OR CHOCOLATE? — POPCORN?

WHAT WOULD YOU SAY?

Hindsight is a wonderful thing; and if you could step back in time what would YOU say to your younger self?

WE ASK THE WOMEN WHO INSPIRE US TO OFFER SOME WORDS OF WISDOM TO THEIR YOUNGER SELVES...

Dear Layne

LIGHTEN UP! Aspiring to be the fittest and most driven successful surfer in the world is your journey. Do not project these same expectations onto your friends and family. Your tenacity is a wonderful advantage but always remember to take full responsibility for your choices by asking probing questions, accept feedback, surround yourself with positive, supportive and honest people and remember that all mistakes are valuable learning opportunities.

Your health is your wealth. Never take it for granted. Learn to cook. A lack of knowledge and skill causes uncertainty, so replace the vegemite sandwiches with a variety of healthy, fresh, seasonal produce to enhance your physical, mental and emotional well being. Success doesn't have to be a struggle. **Have fun!** Trust in your ability and instincts.

Always Be kind to yourself. Always Believe in yourself.

Layne Beachley
Professional surfer and 7 x World Champion

Dearest Kimberly,

Hello and how are you, dear one?

I'm writing you because I can feel some major stress and worry on you. Worry you think you can hide about how you look and how you are, but I can see it! I want you to know you don't have to be so worried about your body, your appearance ... or anything. PLEASE take a minute and recognise you real beauty. BEAUTY in those kind eyes and simply because you are truly a good person. Your hair is wavy, and not straight. Your eyes are not as round as the other girls, but that's OKAY. You don't have to try to be like everyone else. I am proud of you. You are a good person. You are AMAZING just as you are, because you are you! I know sometimes you feel you don't measure up, or that you don't fit in or that you aren't good enough. But shift thinking that way! YOU are perfect just as you are.

Yes, perfect.

Perfectly imperfect!

Believe in yourself.
Believe in your uniqueness.
You are going to be able to help people, and work on things that really mean something to you, once you really start believing in yourself.

I LOVE & accept you just as you are.

All my love,

Kimberly xo

Kimberly Snyder
New York Times bestselling author of The Beauty Detox Power and nutritionist for the mind, body and soul

Lisa Messenger

CEO and creative director of The Messenger group, as well as founder and Editor-in-Chief of The Renegade Collective Magazine

Dear Chrissy "Kissy"

Great news, you're still dancing! It's not exactly how you imagined, but your point shoes have a cozy place in your gym bag. Continue to leap through life.

You're a _free_ spirit. Don't let anyone try to cage you. Live FREE; unbound by fear. Make your own rules. (There will be one man with the strength : confidence to handle you - marry him.)

Be BRAVE, be ADVENTUROUS & GO FOR IT everytime! If it scares you, do it. Go so hard, so passionately, that you wipe out. You're greatest growth will come from brief setbacks.

There are a few difficult times ahead, but have faith that they too shall pass. You will use those moments to bless others.

FORGIVE those who hurt you. Don't harbor anger, sadness or hate - it's only poison to your own soul. Be an example of LOVE and LIGHT.

HEALTH is your greatest wealth. Keep experimenting with your fitness, start doing push-ups, eat more vegetables, and meditate.

A letter to my younger self —

Be strong. And don't be afraid. For no one knows what they are doing any more than you. Life is going to be tough and will throw crazy curve balls at you; ones beyond your control and they'll come when you least expect them.

BUT, it's the rockier parts of our journey that make us stronger, more self-aware and ultimately, more grateful. It's how you react to those curve balls which make us authentic and the best version of yourself. So, hold yourself with grace, humility, strength and courage. Trust yourself. Back yourself. And get up when you fall.

Never forget that life is a revolving door of opportunities. Stay open because they are everywhere. Respect the doors when they close but ALWAYS look for a new, or another way forward.

And don't fall into the trap of worrying about what others think of you. Find your purpose so you can live your 'why' and make a powerful mark on this world.

Be outrageous. Live daringly and OUT LOUD. Dance. Celebrate. Laugh. Make friends. Hug your family. Spread kindness. Enjoy every MOMENT.

And above all else, be grateful for everything.
    For it makes you who you ARE.

            x Lisa Messenger

Become yourself as fully as possible. Take time for meditation in order to hear your purpose. Follow your 'instinct', the joy of your ♡. When you are on the right path, it will be easy and fun.

LAUGH a lot, kiss mom & dad, and pack your bags for a great adventure. You have a BLESSED LIFE - never forget where your blessings came from.
            ♡ Christine Bullock xoxo

P.S. Wear sunscreen, they haven't invented a machine to erase time yet & recycle.

ALWAYS REMEMBER THAT THE PARTS OF YOUR BODY THAT FRUSTRATE OR SADDEN YOU ARE SIMPLY MESSENGERS ASKING YOU TO EAT, DRINK, MOVE, THINK, BREATHE, BELIEVE OR PERCEIVE IN A NEW WAY. SEE THEM AS THE GIFT THAT THEY ARE.

            ♡ LIBBY

Now... what would you say to your younger self?

Beauty

[BEAU'TY] NOUN

A grace in the heart, a light in the soul,
a twinkle in the eye, a magic in the mind.

Beauty is an authenticity that cannot be seen, it
can only be felt. Beauty is the words you speak,
the kindness you share, the happiness you feel
and the passion you project. Beauty is being you.

SHE IS BEAUTY.

IT'S IN HER EYES, IN HER SMILE AND
INHERENTLY IN HER SOUL.

IT'S NOT A LOOK, IT'S A FEELING AND IT
STARTED THE MINUTE SHE DECIDED TO BE
EXACTLY WHO SHE IS.

SHE DOESN'T PLACE IMPORTANCE ON
STANDARDS OR IDEALS, BUT RATHER ON
CULTIVATING NURTURING RITUALS THAT
MAKE HER FEEL HER MOST BEAUTIFUL.

SHE BELIEVES IN THE EASE OF SIMPLICITY
AND IS ALL ABOUT ENHANCING, NOT HIDING.

HER BEAUTY IS RAW AND REAL AND IT'S IN
EVERYTHING SHE DOES.

the MNB beauty

commandments

1. Thou shalt always remove
   make-up before bed

2. Thou shalt always celebrate
   your unique individuality

3. Thou shalt always protect
   your skin with SPF+

4. Thou shalt never compare
   yourself to anybody else

5. Thou shalt nourish from the inside out

6. Thou shalt smile every day

7. Thou shalt get 8 hours of sleep a night

8. Thou shalt embrace your
   natural beauty

9. Thou shalt abolish all self doubt

10. Thou shalt love the skin you're in

BE WHO YOU ARE

66 THERE IS NOTHING
MORE RARE, NOR MORE
BEAUTIFUL, THAN
A WOMAN BEING
UNAPOLOGETICALLY
HERSELF; COMFORTABLE
IN HER PERFECT
IMPERFECTION. TO ME,
THAT IS THE TRUE ESSENCE
OF BEAUTY. 99

STEVE MARABOLI

BE YOUR OWN KIND OF
BEAUTIFUL

We know you've heard it a hundred times before, and despite how clichéd it sounds, beauty is more than skin deep. It's one of the very first lessons we're taught in life by our mothers and grandmothers, yet more often than not, it's also one of the first lessons we seem to forget. Each and every woman who wanders this planet is unique, fascinating and completely irreplaceable, and you know what? Each and every one of us is just as beautiful.

We live in a culture that's obsessed with the quest for perfection, and we all know at times its standards are unattainable and even a little removed from reality, but what really defines beauty? Magazines? Celebrities? Cosmetic companies? No, no and no... YOU define beauty.

Women are inherently beautiful souls, but we're sensitive ones too. It can be hard to ignore what society is feeding us, which all too often leads to comparison; that all-consuming complex that can wreak havoc on our sense of self worth. 'I wish I had her thighs', 'that top looks better on her than it does on me', 'why isn't my stomach as flat as hers?'... do any of those sound familiar? Stop girl, because you are amazing and you are enough. Our uniqueness is what makes this world such a beautiful and interesting place... can you imagine how monotonous life would seem if we all walked and talked the same?

They say comparison is the thief of joy, so instead of wasting your days wishing for something another woman has, try spending a little bit of time appreciating yourself and loving what you have... you're pretty special you know! There is nothing more inspiring than a woman who is 100% comfortable in her own skin, and that means not only celebrating the shiny, sparkly things you like about yourself, but also the cute and unique little quirks that really make you, you!

As women, we need to reframe the conversation we're having with ourselves, because for every quality you're wishing for in someone else, they're probably wishing for one of yours too, whether it be your sparkling personality or eternal sense of optimism. The grass isn't greener on the other side... it's greener where you water it, so instead of zoning in on what you don't like about your pale skin or timid nature, focus on finding a reason you love it.

Just like a good heart, true beauty is an enchanting energy that shines from the inside out and it's the kind that's enhanced by honesty and authenticity, not filters or make-up. So pour yourself a big glass of self love, it will make you happier and more beautiful than any diet ever will.

> "REJOICE AND LOVE YOURSELF TODAY 'CAUSE BABY YOU WERE BORN THIS WAY."
> -LADY GAGA

BEING BEAUTIFUL IS BEING YOU!

THERE IS NOTHING MORE INSPIRING

xx

BEAU-TEA BLENDS

GINGER, CACAO, PEPPERMINT & CINNAMON BLEND

SERVES 4
PREP TIME: 1 MINUTE
TOTAL TIME: 5 MINUTES

YOU WILL NEED:

7 CUPS (1.75 LITRES) OF WATER
1 TEASPOON CACAO NIBS
1 TEASPOON DESICCATED COCONUT
1 HEAPED TABLESPOON (20G) CHOPPED RAISINS
1 TEASPOON GROUND CINNAMON
1 TABLESPOON ORGANIC DRIED
½ CUP (180G) RAW ORGANIC HONEY
2 TABLESPOONS LOOSE PEPPERMINT TEA LEAVES
1 TABLESPOON ORGANIC DRIED ROSE PETAL FOR GARNISH

THIS IS HOW WE DO IT:

PLACE ALL INGREDIENTS, IN A SAUCEPAN OVER MEDIUM HEAT. BRING TO BOIL.

SIMMER FOR 3 MINUTES.
SET ASIDE FOR 2 MINUTES TO INFUSE.

STRAIN INTO A TEAPOT OR HEATPROOF JUG.

GARNISH WITH DRIED ROSE PETALS

LEMON, VANILLA & MINT BLEND

SERVES 4
PREP TIME: 5 MINUTES
TOTAL TIME: 8 MINUTES

YOU WILL NEED:

1 ORGANIC LEMON
1 VANILLA BEAN, SPLIT LENGTHWAYS, SEEDS SEPARATED
1/2 CUP FIRMLY PACKED FRESH MINT LEAVES
1/2 CUP (175g) HONEY
7 CUPS (1.75 LITRES) WATER
2 TABLESPOONS BLACK TEA LEAVES

THIS IS HOW WE DO IT:

USE A ZESTER OR A VEGETABLE PEELER & A SMALL SHARP KNIFE TO CUT THE LEMON RIND INTO THIN STRIPS.

CUT 6 THIN SLICES FROM THE LEMON & CUT EACH IN HALF.

PLACE THE LEMON RIND, LEMON, VANILLA BEAN AND SEEDS, MINT, HONEY & WATER IN A SAUCEPAN OVER MEDIUM HEAT. BRING TO BOIL.

SIMMER FOR 5 MINUTES.
ADD TEA LEAVES. COVER.
SET ASIDE FOR 3 MINUTES TO INFUSE.
STRAIN INTO A TEAPOT OR HEATPROOF JUG.

SERVE WITH EXTRA MINT LEAVES & LEMON SLICES IF DESIRED.

active amino hair mask

FROM ROOT TO TIP, COAT YOUR LOCKS IN
THIS NOURISHING PROTEIN-PACKED MASK
THAT WILL REPAIR, POLISH AND SHINE.

MAKES: ⅔ CUP OR 1 HAIR MASK
PREP TIME: 5 MINUTES

YOU WILL NEED:

- <u>1</u> TABLESPOON COCONUT OIL
- 1/4 MEDIUM AVOCADO (62g)
- <u>1</u> RAW EGG

THIS IS HOW WE DO IT:

COMBINE ALL INGREDIENTS &
MIX THROUGH DRY HAIR,
COATING EACH STRAND.
LEAVE FOR ONE HOUR.

WASH AS PER NORMAL ENSURING
THE ENTIRE HAIR MASK
IS REMOVED.

ADD A TEASPOON OF
HONEY FOR EXTRA LUSCIOUS LOCKS.

YOU WILL NEED:

1 CUP (220g) RAW SUGAR
1/2 CUP (125g) COCONUT OIL
3 TABLESPOONS DESICCATED COCONUT
2-3 TABLESPOONS GROUND COFFEE
2 TABLESPOONS CACAO POWDER

all over body

BEAUTY SCRUB

THE PERFECT MORNING PICK-ME-UP THAT WILL LEAVE YOUR SKIN
FEELING REFRESHED, VIBRANT & SILKY SMOOTH.

PREP TIME: 10 MINUTES
MAKES: 1½ CUPS

THIS IS HOW WE DO IT:

MIX ALL INGREDIENTS TOGETHER
WELL & STORE IN AN AIRTIGHT JAR.

TO USE -
MASSAGE 2 TABLESPOONS OF THE
MIXTURE ONTO SKIN.

v

LATHER WELL

v

RINSE!

FACE TIME

NOURISHING FAVOURS TO HELP YOU PUT
YOUR BEST FACE FORWARD.

MIRACLE MOISTURISER

Prep time: 10 minutes
Makes: 1 cup

YOU WILL NEED:

3/4 CUP (180 ml) COCONUT OIL
2 TABLESPOONS ALOE VERA GEL
8-10 DROPS PEPPERMINT ESSENTIAL OIL

THIS IS HOW WE DO IT:

ADD ALL INGREDIENTS IN A BOWL
USING A HAND MIXER WITH
A WHISK ATTACHMENT,
WHIP UNTIL A SMOOTH, CREAMY
EMULSION FORMS.

HONEY COCONUT FACE MASK

Prep time: 10 minutes
Makes: ½ cup

YOU WILL NEED:

1 TABLESPOON HONEY
1 TABLESPOON NATURAL YOGURT
1 TEASPOON CINNAMON
2 TEASPOONS DESSICATED COCONUT

THIS IS HOW WE DO IT:

MIX TOGETHER
˅ SPREAD OVER FACE
˅ LEAVE FOR 20 MINUTES
˅ WASH

NATURAL LIP JAM

DRY LIPS NEED COMFORT TOO. PUCKER UP WITH
THIS 100% NATURAL CREATION FORMULATED TO HEAL,
REPAIR AND MOISTURISE.

Prep Time: 5 Minutes. Makes: ¼ cup

YOU WILL NEED:

2 TABLESPOONS HONEY
2 TABLESPOONS COCONUT OIL
   (MELTED)
1 TEASPOON CRANBERRY or
   BERRY POWDER
2 DROPS VITAMIN E OIL
2 DROPS ROSE WATER

THIS IS HOW WE DO IT:

COMBINE ALL INGREDIENTS IN A
SMALL GLASS JAR, LET COOL
AND APPLY TO LIPS FOR A
NON TOXIC LIP GLOSS ALTERNATIVE.

ahh yum!

TRUE BEAUTY COMES
FROM KNOWING, ACCEPTING
AND BEING YOURSELF.
THE MORE YOU SHOW WHO
YOU REALLY ARE, THE MORE
BEAUTIFUL YOU BECOME

LORNA JANE CLARKSON

URISH

Nourish. It is arguably one of our favourite things to do, and we simply cannot stop learning more and more about it. Whether it's picking up fresh finds from our local farmers' market, discovering new, exciting ways to turn naughty foods nice, or packing our plate with an abundance of nutrients, in our eyes, when it comes to nourishing our bodies, inspiration is limitless.

WHEN IT COMES TO NOURISHING...

write your own rules

Despite all the fad diets, meal-replacing shakes and super detox programs out there promising you thinner thighs, leaner bodies and youthful radiance - we know that when it comes to nourishing our bodies; there is no one-size-fits-all way to do it!

We are all individuals with unique tastes and dietary requirements, so looking at another person's plate (or body for that matter) and comparing it to our own is pointless. Who says you need to adhere to a strict guideline to be considered healthy? Who says you need to label yourself? Who says you can't practise moderation by having a little bit of what you love when you want it?

We say, rather than arming yourself with a hard set of do's and dont's, why not try opening your mind to new health promoting foods – super delicious ingredients that YOU choose without any stress or guilt attached.

We say, eat when you're hungry and stop when you're full.

We say, swap that sugary confection for something more nourishing, like honey-coated nuts.

We say, if you want to be healthier, try new foods until you find the flavour you love. If your breakfast gets you through to lunch, listen to your body and don't reach for snacks if you're not actually hungry!

We say, add colour to your diet, eat rainbows, choose nutrients over calories, keep hydrated, load up on leafy greens for lunch and dinner, embrace whole foods, include protein in every meal with a side of healthy fats like coconut, seeds, nuts, avocado or even fish. We say, have fun with fermenting, chew your food, and make smart swaps.

What do you say?

We encourage you to create your very own nourish style, so you can prove to yourself once and for all that you can be healthy, and still enjoy food without having to go from crash diet to new fad and back again.

Be a nourishing rockstar... write your own rules and have a hell of a good time being healthy.

Create your own food pyramid!

HOW TO BUILD THE PERFECT PLATE

GONE ARE THE DAYS OF COUNTING CALORIES... AND GOOD RIDDANCE WE SAY!

Calories are complex little creatures that far too many people place far too much importance on, but we're here to set your plate straight! When you choose to nourish with real food in its most natural state, your body knows exactly what to do with it - no counting or subtracting involved!

Contrary to popular belief, the secret to good health is not found in counting calories, nor is it in restricting food groups. The secret to good health is about being mindful of your macros: powerful protein, healthy fats and wholesome carbohydrates.

The best place to start is by adding in so much good, you crowd out the bad.

This is a gradual step and can be applied to any meal, any mood, any sweet or savoury tooth. So, start with a rule of thirds and base your plate around the macro groups. Include options from each, and apply this to every meal. This doesn't mean you have to say goodbye to what you love. Those tastebuds still need to be tantalised and the key is to choose healthier options to replace the nasty ones you may have formerly favoured. We guarantee that counting macros over calories will foster a longer, happier and healthy life.

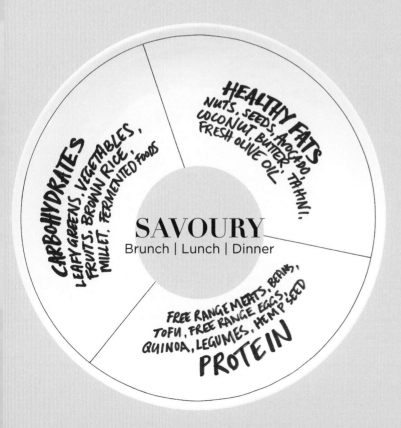

HEALTHY FATS NUTS, SEEDS, AVOCADO, COCONUT, BUTTER, TAHINI, FRESH OLIVE OIL

CARBOHYDRATES LEAFY GREENS, VEGETABLES, FRUITS, BROWN RICE, MILLET, FERMENTED FOODS

PROTEIN FREE RANGE MEATS, BEANS, TOFU, FREE RANGE EGGS, QUINOA, LEGUMES, HEMP SEED

SAVOURY
Brunch | Lunch | Dinner

HEALTHY FATS NUTS, DARK CHOCOLATE, NUT BUTTERS, FLAXSEED, COCONUT

CARBOHYDRATES OATS, FRUIT, PUFFED MILLET, HONEY, MAPLE, SPELT FLOUR

PROTEIN FULL FAT YOGHURT, BUCKWHEAT, CHIA SEEDS, QUINOA, NUT MYLKS

SWEET
Breakfast | Snack | Dessert

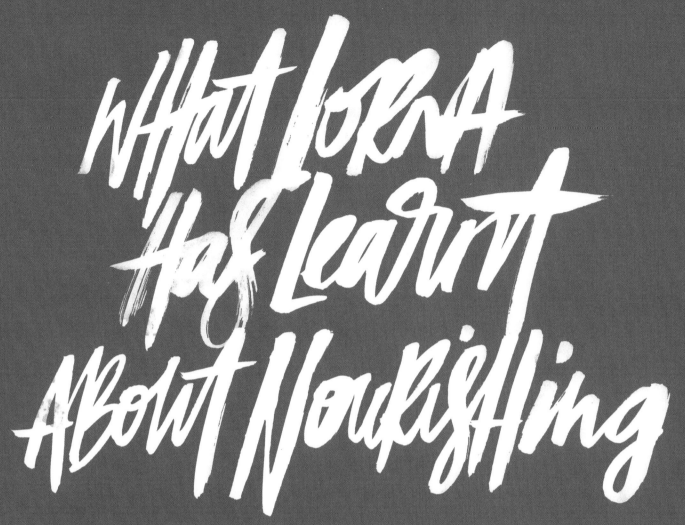

WHAT LORNA HAS LEARNT ABOUT NOURISHING

BE INSPIRED TO UP YOUR 'NOURISHING' GAME
WITH LORNA JANE CLARKSON

1. Ditch Dieting & Write Your Own Rules
We inherently know what our bodies need, we just need to honour ourselves and create our own rules based on how we want to live our lives. Food is your friend so choose foods that make you feel amazing and complement your lifestyle.

2. Chew Chew Chew
I know it can be difficult at times, but make it a rule to sit down and savour your food whenever possible. If you can, chew each mouthful 15 - 20 times to improve digestion, increase nutritional uptake and savour and enjoy your delicious meal.

3. Count Macros not Calories
Macros (or macronutrients) are the proteins, fats and carbohydrates that make up the food we eat. So when I say 'count them' it's more about being aware - if you had a high-carb breakfast of oats and fruit in the morning, then be sure to get some proteins and fats into your meals for the rest of the day – simple really!

4. Why Water
We know you're sick of hearing the 2 litre a day thing! But the truth is, water makes you gorgeous! It moisturises and hydrates your skin, is essential for maintaining your skin's elasticity, keeps your digestion and metabolism working properly and would have to be the best and purest weight-loss tool on the planet – so drink up!

5. Attack Snacking
Eating a little less on a more regular basis (every 3-4 hours) boosts your metabolism, keeps you focused, puts your body into fat-burning mode and helps keep those pesky sugar cravings at bay.

6. Miss it? Then Swap It
So you feel like you're missing out on all the fun by deciding to eat well! Why not find healthy alternatives for all of your unhealthy cravings and learn to look forward to guilt-free treats that nourish your body? Some of my favourites are: dates instead of candy, blended frozen banana instead of ice-cream and baked sweet potato chips instead of fries. (See page 76 for our amazing MNB suggestions).

AN ODE TO BREAKFAST

Breakfast. Two little syllables that get us far too excited and bounding out of bed to break the fast is probably our favourite thing to do. Not only is it (in our humble opinion) the most important meal of the day, but arguably the most delicious. We believe that everyday is another chance to get it right, and it's the rituals you choose to live by that essentially define the person you become. Just like morning meditation or brushing your teeth, breakfast is an essential component that you just should not skip out on. And why would you want to? Whether it's in the form of a smoothie bowl resembling the colours of the rainbow; or a classic soft boiled egg with all the humble accompaniments, in our eyes breakfast inspiration is limitless. In short breakfast, you're a treat, everytime we meet... even if it's for dinner.

□□□

BREAKFAST CRUMBLE

SERVES: 4 | PREP + COOK TIME: 50 MINUTES

*A crumble doesn't just have to be the finale to a great evening meal but can
also be the opening act to a beautiful breakfast!*

YOU WILL NEED:

FRUIT FILLING

400g (12.5oz) red rhubarb, trimmed,
  cut into 2.5cm pieces
½ teaspoon vanilla extract
1/ 3 cup honey or maple syrup
½ cup (125ml) orange juice
2½ cups (360g) mixed berries

CRUMBLE TOPPING

½ cup (100g) quinoa flakes
½ cup (45g) steel cut rolled oats
pinch of salt
4 pitted medjool dates, chopped
2½ tablespoons coconut oil

THIS IS HOW WE DO IT:

Preheat oven to 190°C/350°F Grease a 6
cup/1.5 litre baking dish with coconut oil.

Place rhubarb in a dish and mix in vanilla,
honey and orange juice. Stir in the berries.

In a separate bowl, combine quinoa
flakes, oats and salt. Add dates and
coconut oil and mix until large crumbs
are formed. Sprinkle the crumble over
the fruit mixture evenly and bake for 30
minutes or until the juices are bubbling
and crumble is browned.

NUTRITIONAL COUNT PER SERVE
14.4g total fat (11g saturated fat);
71.8g carbohydrate; 7.2g protein; 7.6g fibre

QUINOA VANILLA PUDDING

SERVES 4 | PREP + COOK TIME: 45 MINUTES

*If you want to put a fresh spin on an old classic, this delicious
quinoa pudding will do just the trick…*

YOU WILL NEED:

1 litre cocnut mylk
1 teaspoon vanilla bean paste
¼ cup (55g) coconut sugar
pinch of salt
1 cup (200g) uncooked white quinoa
½ cup passionfruit pulp (6 passionfruits)
2 tablespoons coconut flakes

THIS IS HOW WE DO IT:

In a small saucepan on medium heat, bring coconut mylk,
sugar, salt and vanilla to a simmer. Add quinoa, reduce to
low heat and cook for about 30 minutes. Once the quinoa is
cooked and liquid thickened, remove from heat and allow to
cool slightly. Layer the quinoa and most of the passionfruit
pulp into bowls or jars.

Sprinkle with remaining fresh passionfruit and coconut
flakes. Serve immediately. Can be stored in the fridge and
eaten cold.

NUTRITIONAL COUNT PER SERVE
48.3g total fat (41g saturated fat); 53.3g carbohydrate;
12.6g protein; 5.2g fibre

Corn
FRITTERS
with avocado & goat's cheese salsa

MAKES 12 | PREP + COOK TIME: 35 MINUTES

Feel fresh and fancy with a nourishing twist on a familiar favourite, fritters are back with flare.

YOU WILL NEED:

FRITTERS

1 small (90g) zucchini, grated
2 cups fresh corn kernels (2 fresh cobs)
½ cup (75g) chickpea flour (besan)
3 free range eggs, whisked
2 garlic cloves, minced
1 spring onion, thinly sliced
Himalayan rock salt
black pepper (to taste)
coconut oil for frying

SALSA

1 medium (250g) avocado
2 tablespoons goat's cheese
1½ tablespoons lemon juice
(½ a lemon is fine)
¼ cup chopped coriander or parsley
fresh coriander leaves, to garnish

THIS IS HOW WE DO IT:

Combine grated zucchini and corn kernels in a bowl. In a separate bowl whisk the flour and remaining ingredients, except for oil until there are no lumps. Combine the flour mixture with the zucchini and corn and mix well.

Heat coconut oil in a fry pan on medium heat. Spoon heaped tablespoons of batter into the fry pan and leave enough space between each fritter to flip them.

Fry for 3-4 minutes each side. When cooked and browned on both sides, remove fritters from heat and onto a plate lined with paper towel. Combine all salsa ingredients in a mixing bowl and mash with a fork.

Stack the cooked corn fritters with a layer of salsa between. Garnish with extra fresh coriander.

NUTRITIONAL COUNT PER SERVE
19.7g total fat (6.6g saturated fat); 21.5g carbohydrate; 17.5g protein; 5.7g fibre

I'VE
99 PRO
BUT NOU
AIN'T

GOT
BLEMS.
—
RISHING
ONE

WE SAY...

CHOOSE **ZOODLES** NOT **PASTA**

SWAP DONUTS FOR FAUXNUTS

MILK CHOC NOT **DARK**

WE DIG **PINK**

DITCH THE TABLE SALT

HOLD THE **Latte**

GO! GREEN JUICE

76

SWAP THIS
FOR THAT

Many people think that in order to be healthy, you have to deprive yourself of your favourite foods. But how mundane would that make mealtime?

Deprivation
is a slippery slope that can lead to loads of other problems, so it's time to ditch the dreaded 'D' word
and embrace the smart swap!

We are constantly inspired by finding new ways to nourish, even more so when we can find a way to turn a tasty treat from naughty ▬ to nice.▬

FACT

You don't need to stop it,
just swap it for the good stuff.

See our fave 'swaps' on the following pages...

FISH BURRITO

YOU WILL NEED:

FISH

4 fillets (800g) firm white fish
1½ teaspoons smoked paprika
1 teaspoon garlic powder
1 teaspoon dried oregano
1 teaspoon onion powder
½ teaspoon cumin
½ teaspoon salt
½ teaspoon cayenne pepper
2 tablespoons extra virgin olive oil
1 cob of corn, kernels removed
1 can (425g) black beans,
   rinsed and drained

SLAW (MAKES 8 CUPS)

½ medium (600g) red cabbage,
   finely shredded
¼ medium (300g) green cabbage,
   finely shredded
½ medium (85g) red onion, diced finely
½ punnet (125g) cherry tomatoes,
   sliced in half
½ cup coarsely chopped fresh coriander
1 tablespoon lime juice

AVOCADO SAUCE

½ cup (140g) goat's or Greek yogurt
   or tahini
1 medium (250g) avocado, pitted and
   peeled
¼ cup fresh coriander, chopped
1 ½ tablespoons lime juice
1 jalapeno, seeded, chopped
salt, to taste

2 cups (400g) brown rice,
cooked, to serve

BOWL
SERVES 4
PREP + COOK TIME: 50 MINUTES

*Fake-out the take-out with these
completely customisable burrito
bowls sans the gluten.*

THIS IS HOW WE DO IT:

In a small bowl, combine smoked paprika, garlic powder, dried oregano, onion powder, cumin, salt and cayenne pepper. Sprinkle fillets and rub in. Heat 1 tablespoon of the olive oil in a large non-stick skillet over medium-high heat. Add fish and fry 3 minutes per side. Check the middle of the fish. It should flake easily and be opaque throughout.

Remove from the skillet and set aside. Cover with foil to keep warm. If necessary, add remaining oil to the pan and add the corn. Cook over high heat, stirring occasionally, until crisp. Add black beans and heat through.

Combine all the Avocado Sauce ingredients in food processor or blender. Pulse until well-combined. Combine all slaw ingredients in a large bowl and mix well. Layer rice, bean mixture, and Slaw in a serving bowl. Top with fish, avocado sauce and extra lime juice if desired.

NUTRITIONAL COUNT PER SERVE
28g total fat (6g saturated fat); 104.4g carbohydrate;
62.8g protein; 20.7g fibre

crumbed chicken
BURGER BOARD
w/ miso slaw

SERVES: 2 | PREP + COOK TIME: 45 MINS

"Scrap the bun and have some fun, there's no need to gobble your burger with a side of guilt anymore."

YOU WILL NEED:

1 egg
¼ cup nutritional yeast flakes
½ cup (60g) almond meal
2 fillets (400g) free range chicken breast
1-2 stalks (40g) kale, de-stemmed and chopped
½ apple, julienned
watercress (for garnish)
1 tablespoon coconut oil (for frying)
lemon wedges, to serve

MISO SLAW

½ cup (140g) full-fat Greek yoghurt
2 tablespoons red or yellow miso
2 teaspoons fresh grated ginger
1 garlic clove, minced
1 teaspoon sesame oil
2 teaspoons tamari
3 cups (240g) finely shredded red cabbage
1 carrot, julienned
1 spring onion, thinly sliced

THIS IS HOW WE DO IT:

In a small bowl, crack the egg and whisk well with 1 tablespoon of water. Combine nutritional yeast and almond meal on a medium plate. Cut each breast in half lengthways to form 2 thin fillets. Dip the pieces in the egg, then the almond meal, and nutritional yeast mixture.

Heat the coconut oil in a fry pan on a medium heat. Fry the chicken breasts on each side for about 4 minutes until cooked through. Set aside to assemble burger bowl.

MAKE THE SLAW

Whisk Greek yoghurt, miso, ginger, garlic, sesame oil and tamari in a bowl until combined. Toss with cabbage, carrot and spring onion.

To serve, in a bowl, lay out the leafy greens, kale, apple and slaw. Slice chicken into strips and lay on top. Serve with sourdough bun or roasted sweet potato and rosemary wedges.

NUTRITIONAL COUNT PER SERVE
41.3g total fat (15g saturated fat); 36g carbohydrate; 81g protein; 12.8g fibre

"The apple of my pie… eat easy with this flan-tastic sweet bake."

APPLE PIE

SERVES: 4 | PREP + COOK TIME: 1 HOUR

YOU WILL NEED:

CRUST

50g (1.7oz) grass fed butter, chopped
2 tablespoons rapadura sugar
3 cups (360g) almond meal
1 egg
1 tablespoon finely grated lemon rind
½ teaspoon vanilla bean paste
½ teaspoon ground cinnamon
pinch of Himalayan rock salt
coconut oil (for greasing baking dish)
pie dish (approx. 18cm pie plate)

FILLING

1 tablespoon coconut oil
5 medium apples (750g)
   peeled and slice
1 tablespoon honey
¼ cup (60ml) lemon juice
20g (0.7oz) grass fed butter
½ teaspoon vanilla bean paste
½ teaspoon ground cinnamon
pinch of Himalayan rock salt
½ punnet (40g) fresh or frozen
   raspberries

THIS IS HOW WE DO IT:

Preheat oven to 190°C/350°F and grease pie dish with coconut oil. Whip butter and rapadura together until smooth. Gently blend in almond meal, egg and remaining crust ingredients. Once the mixture has started to look like rough dough, keep 2 large tablespoons aside to create the letters on top. Press the remaining dough over the base and sides of the baking tin. Bake for 10-12 minutes until golden. Remove from oven and allow to cool.

Place all fillings except raspberries in a saucepan on low heat. Cover and bring the mixture to a gentle boil. Reduce heat and cook for 5 minutes until there is no liquid left, stirring occasionally. Stir through raspberries until combined. Let the mixture cool slightly. Remove apples with a slotted spoon or drain in colander and layer evenly over the crust.

From the pastry you have set aside, cut out your choice of words from a stencil and lay flat over the pastry. Assemble over the top of the pie.

Bake for 10 minutes. Serve hot. Suitable for freezing.

NUTRITIONAL COUNT PER SERVE
69.9g total fat (16.8g saturated fat); 35.3g carbohydrate; 20.9g protein; 12g fibre

Nice Cream

Who says you need to give up ice cream? Just make it N-I-C-E

MAKES: 6 CUPS | PREP + COOK TIME: 15 MINUTES PER FLAVOUR + STANDING TIME
NICE CREAM NEEDS TO SIT OUT OF THE FREEZER FOR 30 MINUTES BEFORE SERVING

COTTON CANDY

2 frozen (400g) medium bananas
1 cup (250ml) coconut mylk
2 tablespoons of dried
  cranberry or berry powder
1 tablespoon dried goji berries
1-2 tablespoons coconut flakes
2 cups ice

In a blender, process bananas, mylk, berry powder and ice. Once smooth, fold in goji berries until just combined. Sprinkle with coconut flakes.

Pour into container and leave to set in freezer.

13.4g total fat (11.9g saturated fat); 15.3g carbohydrate; 2g protein; 1.6g fibre

TIP:
Combine cacao, cocoa butter and honey for a choc drizzle on page 167

MINT CHOC CHIP

1 frozen (200g) medium banana
1 cup baby spinach leaves
2 tablespoons honey or maple syrup
2 tablespoons dark chocolate
  chips or cacao nibs
½ tablespoon peppermint extract
1 cup (250ml) can coconut mylk,
  chilled in the fridge for 3 hours
2 cups ice

Place all the ingredients (except for the cacao nibs and peppermint extract) in a high speed blender until thick and smooth. Add in the peppermint extract and mix until just combined. Add the cacao or dark choc chips last and fold through.

Pour into container and leave to set in freezer.

12.2g total fat (10.2g saturated fat); 22.2g carbohydrate; 2g protein; 1g fibre

CHOC CRUNCH

1 cup coconut flesh from
  2 young coconuts (save the
  coconut water for pre or post
  workout electrolyte drink)
2 frozen (400g) medium bananas
¼ cup (25g) cacao powder
1 tablespoon almond butter
2 teaspoons maple syrup
½ teaspoon vanilla bean paste
Pinch of sea salt
2 cups of ice (depending
  on thickness)
1 tablespoon cacao nibs

Process all ingredients (except the cacao nibs) in a food processor or blender until combined. Fold through cacao nibs last with a spoon and top with additional nibs.

Pour into container and leave to set in freezer.

12.8g total fat (6.3g saturated fat); 15.6g carbohydrate; 4.6g protein; 3.4g fibre

I SCREAM, YOU SCREAM, WE ALL SCREAM

What you won't
Find in a
MNB
Girls
Kitchen

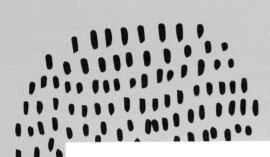

1. WHITE SUGAR

2. LOW FAT ANYTHING - JUST EAT THE REAL THING.

3. FIZZY DRINKS - BECAUSE WE HAVE KOMBUCHA BREWING.

4. VEGETABLE OIL - A STRICT 'NO HYDROGENATED OILS ALLOWED' ZONE

5. FROZEN MEALS - YOU KNOW WHAT THEY SAY, FRESH IS BEST.

6. MARGARINE - NOT A FOOD

7. POTATO CHIPS - BECAUSE NOTHING IS BETTER THAN A CRISPY KALE CHIP.

8. CORDIAL - FRESHLY COLD PRESSED JUICE, ANYONE?

9. LOLLIES - BECAUSE WE SNACK ON NATURALLY SWEET FRESH FRUIT.

10. CEREALS IN A BOX - DITCH THE PACKETS OF SUGAR & AIR
    & GET BUSY WITH DIY GRANOLA

11. WHITE BREAD - SAY GOODBYE TO REFINED AND KEEP CULTURED
    WITH SOURDOUGH.

Move it

MOVE IN A WAY THAT MAKES YOU SMILE

BE A
MOVER
& A
SHAKER

NO GOAL WAS EVER MET WITHOUT A LITTLE SWEAT

It's hard to be your best, brightest and bubbliest self without making the time to get your move on. MNB Girls move every day, not because we have to, but because we want to. Believe it or not, exercise is not a chore or a burden we put ourselves through every day just because we think it's the right thing to do. In fact, it's quite the opposite!

We believe you should embark on your sweat session with the same amount of enthusiasm you usually reserve for your morning long black. The glowy confidence that exudes after a workout is contagious, and it inspires those around you to do the same... so get moving!

REASONS WHY WE LOVE TO GET OUR MOVE ON (AND SO SHOULD YOU)

- It helps clear our heads from the clutter accumulated daily
- It gives our skin a better glow than a facial
- It leaves us feeling as refreshed as a glass of lemon water
- It relieves stress like nothing else
- It improves our quality of sleep so we don't have to count sheep
- It gives us endorphins, and endorphins make us happy

HOW TO MAKE IT PART OF YOUR EVERYDAY

We've all heard that saying 'when you love what you do, you'll never work a day in your life', right? But did you know that this universally celebrated mantra doesn't just apply to our careers, but to our move routines too?

Think about it for a minute; if you schedule in a run after work, despite the fact that you don't particularly enjoy running, do you think you're more likely to a.) Lace up and pound the pavement or b.) Spend the day dreaming and scheming a way to talk yourself out of it? Even when we're equipped with the best intentions, so often they fall flat when we project them onto something we don't actually want to do. And that's totally ok; you just have to find a move that makes your heart beat a little faster... because you actually want to do it.

Just like the perfect man, when you find the right move for you, you just know. It will make you feel good, give you confidence and your eyes will light up at the prospect of your next rendezvous.

STEP ONE
START SLOWLY

When introducing anything new to your routine, it's always best to ease your way into it to stop your body from being thrown into shock, especially when it comes to anything physical. Don't run like a bull at a gate and start your first week with bi-daily workouts! Remember, sometimes slow and steady really does win the race.

STEP TWO
FINDING THE RIGHT MOVE

You're not going to get hooked on anything you don't enjoy... do you really think chocolate would be as addictive if it tasted like celery? Even if hundreds wax lyrical about how invigorated they feel after a spin class, you might find it totally and completely mind-numbing. If that's the case, don't fret. If you find something you enjoy doing, it won't feel like a chore and is something you're far more likely to make an integral part of your daily routine. It's all about trial and error.

STEP THREE
PLAN IT AND PEN IT

Once you've found your move, not only will you seriously wonder how you ever lived without it, but you'll also find it so much easier to incorporate into your daily routine. Why? Because you really want to! At the start of each week, sit down with your diary or calendar and schedule your workouts like you would your meetings, that way you can fit them in around your work and social obligations and will probably end up striking the perfect balance. Furthermore, scheduling your workouts is the easiest way to hold yourself accountable... you'd never cancel on your boss, right?

STEP FOUR
SHAKE IT UP

If it ain't broke, don't fix it... right? Wrong! When it comes to derailing a perfectly healthy routine, nothing will kill it quicker than boredom, so always remember to shake up the way you move. Remember that the perfect workout program is the one that combines equal parts strength training, cardio and flexibility. So, if nothing gets in the way of you and your yoga class, why not try incorporating some running and weight training in your week too? You might even surprise yourself at how your technique improves as your strength starts to build.

QUIZ TIME

HOW TO FIND YOUR PERFECT WORKOUT

Is there a happily ever after when it comes to choosing the right move for you? Perhaps. Take the quiz and discover which workout is your match made in heaven.

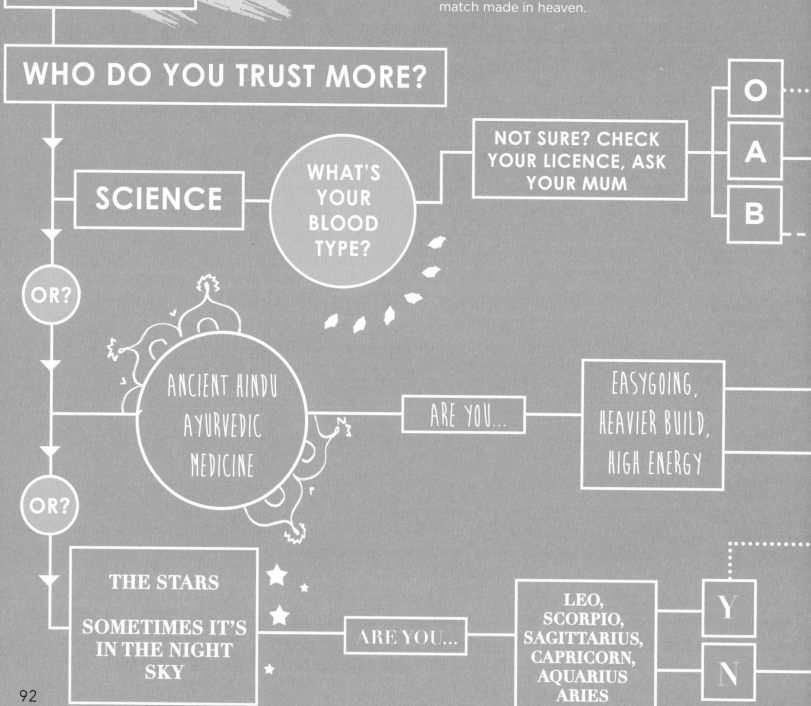

START HERE

WHO DO YOU TRUST MORE?

SCIENCE

WHAT'S YOUR BLOOD TYPE?

NOT SURE? CHECK YOUR LICENCE, ASK YOUR MUM

O
A
B

OR?

ANCIENT HINDU AYURVEDIC MEDICINE

ARE YOU...

EASYGOING, HEAVIER BUILD, HIGH ENERGY

OR?

THE STARS

SOMETIMES IT'S IN THE NIGHT SKY

ARE YOU...

LEO, SCORPIO, SAGITTARIUS, CAPRICORN, AQUARIUS ARIES

Y
N

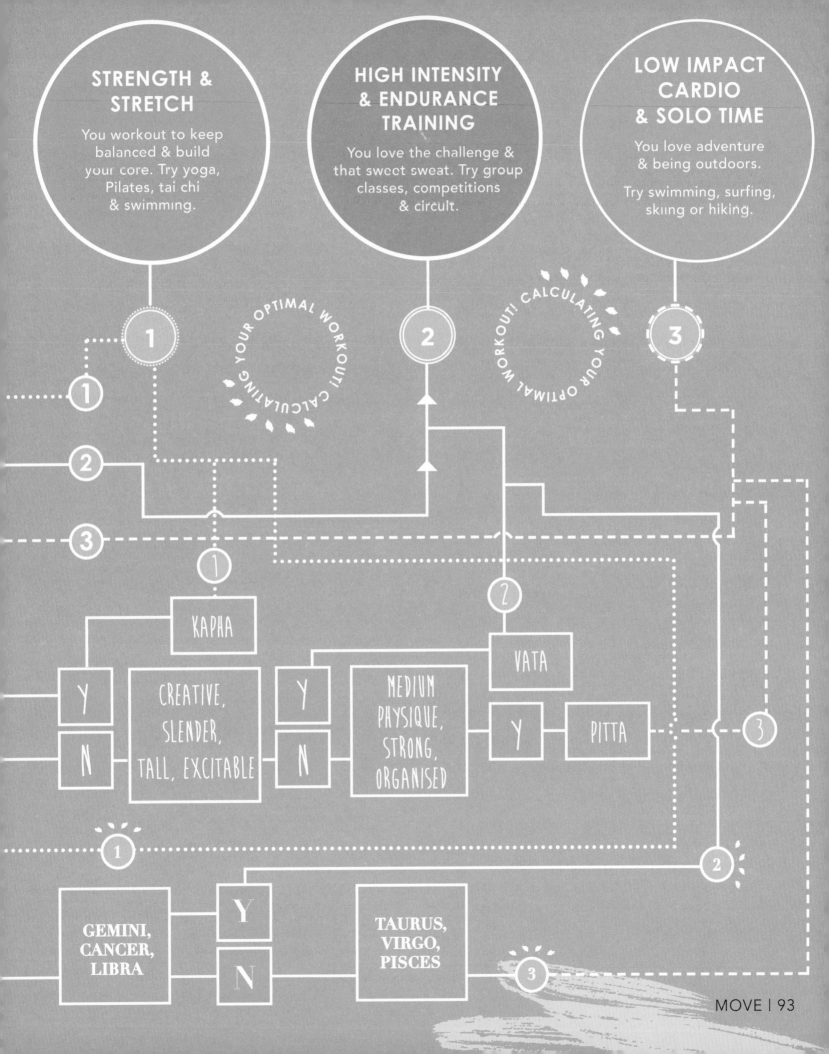

STRENGTH & STRETCH

You workout to keep balanced & build your core. Try yoga, Pilates, tai chi & swimming.

HIGH INTENSITY & ENDURANCE TRAINING

You love the challenge & that sweet sweat. Try group classes, competitions & circuit.

LOW IMPACT CARDIO & SOLO TIME

You love adventure & being outdoors.

Try swimming, surfing, skiing or hiking.

CALCULATING YOUR OPTIMAL WORKOUT!

CALCULATING YOUR OPTIMAL WORKOUT!

KAPHA

CREATIVE, SLENDER, TALL, EXCITABLE

MEDIUM PHYSIQUE, STRONG, ORGANISED

VATA

PITTA

GEMINI, CANCER, LIBRA

TAURUS, VIRGO, PISCES

BE THAT GIRL
WHO WAKES UP WITH
PURPOSE AND INTENT.
BE THAT GIRL
WHO SHOWS UP AND
NEVER GIVES UP.
BE THAT GIRL
WHO BELIEVES
ANYTHING IS POSSIBLE
AND IS WILLING
TO WORK FOR IT.

i JUST MOVE THE WAY I FEEL

Our body is a pretty accurate gauge for our internal wellbeing, so during those times you might be feeling a little stressed and run down, it doesn't mean you have to ditch your sweat session all together, it just means you have to alter it.

96

calm

Whether you want to start your day the balanced way
or soak up some serenity before you hit the hay, these
moves have got you covered.

1. Warm Up: Sun Salutation followed by 20 seconds Child's Pose (repeat 3 times) **2.** Squat (hold 20 seconds,
5 slow Squats) **3.** Right Side Lunge (hold 20 seconds, 5 slow Side Lunges) **4.** Left Side Lunge
(hold 20 seconds, 5 slow Side Lunges) **5.** Plank (hold 20 seconds) Complete 2-3 rounds

STRENGTH

You don't have to spend hours in a gym pumping iron to build strength. Feel stronger in an instant with this hard-hitting yet highly effective sequence.

1. Warm Up: skipping (2-3 minutes) **2.** Sumo Squats **3.** Alternating Lunges **4.** Plank Knee to Elbow **5.** Squat Press **6.** Sit Ups **Round 1** (20 reps of each exercise, rest 30 seconds); **Round 2** (16 reps of each exercise, rest 30 seconds); **Round 3** (12 reps of each exercise, rest 30 seconds); **Round 4** (8 reps of each exercise, rest 30 seconds); **Round 5** (4 reps of each exercise, rest 30 seconds)

ENERGY

If you're lacking a little bit of get up and go, don't reach for another coffee, reach for your sneakers instead and give this workout a red hot go!

1. Warm Up: alternating between High Knees (45 seconds, 20 seconds rest, repeat 3 times)
2. Pop Squats **3.** Alternating Lunges **4.** Push Ups **5.** Mountain Climbers
Round 1 (45 seconds work, 20 seconds rest between exercises); **Round 2** (45 seconds work, 15 seconds rest between exercises); **Round 3** (5 seconds work, 10 seconds rest between exercises)

THE ART OF BUILDING THE PERFECT SMOOTHIE

We can sip them, slurp them and suck them through straws, they delight us with flavours we just can't ignore! We can blend them and mix them and sprinkle them sweet, we just love a good smoothie – it's our favourite pre or post workout treat!

THIS IS HOW WE DO IT

Bee pollen to get you buzzing complete with an extra hit of protein

Mint, maca powder and dates for extra vitamins and minerals

Nut mylk will give you the extra hit of nourishing amino acids

Nut butter to pack in a little protein and a lotta' taste

Greens because they contain magnesium to optimize muscle contraction

Bananas are full of B vitamins, crucial for energy production

Buckwheat on top for added crunch, complete with an extra hit of protein

Cacao powder for added antioxidants and a little taste of guilt free indulgence

Honey to add a spoonful of liquid gold

Sweet cinnamon will balance that blood sugar right out

Always add **coconut water** for extra hydration before your workout

Include two types of protein that will give your muscles the TLC and repair they need

Frozen berries will refuel your body with antioxidants

Take a leaf out of Popeye's book and get your hit of iron with a cup of **spinach**

DELICIOUS EXTRAS

DRY GOES LAST

SWEETEN UP

FAB FLAVOUR

LOVELY LIQUID

PACK IN SOME PROTEIN

FREEZE YOUR FRUIT

PICK YOUR PRODUCE

ICE ICE BABY IS ALWAYS RECOMMENDED TO THICKEN UP YOUR SMOOTHIE

PRE WORKOUT FOR ENERGY

To get the energy you need to conquer that cardio or smash out an extra set of reps

POST WORKOUT TO REPLENISH

To repair that hard working body of yours with the nutrients it needs after your workout.

BLUEBERRY BANOFFEE SMOOTHIE

pre workout

SERVES: 2

PREP TIME:
30 MINUTES

TIP: CHILL COCONUT
CREAM OVERNIGHT

**THE CLASSIC
BANOFFEE
INGREDIENTS:
BANANA, TOFFEE
AND CREAM
ARE HARD
TO BEAT!**

TOFFEE SAUCE
(MAKES 1 CUP)

You will need:

150ml (5oz) coconut mylk
10 pitted medjool dates
2 tablespoons honey

Blend all ingredients together until
a sauce forms. If not thick enough,
add more dates. The sauce will
need to be thick to be drizzled
around the jar/glass.

SMOOTHIE
(MAKES 800ML 127OZ)

You will need:

1½ (300g) frozen bananas
⅔ cup (75g) frozen blueberries
2 cups (500ml) almond mylk
1 teaspoon vanilla bean paste
1 tablespoon almond butter

Blend all ingredients together
in a high-speed blender
until combined.

TOPPING

You will need:
⅔ cup (160ml) coconut cream
  (chilled overnight)
banana slices, to garnish

Chill coconut cream can in the fridge
overnight. The next day, remove the
can from the fridge without tipping or
shaking and remove the lid. Scrape out
the top of thickened cream and leave
the liquid behind (reserve for use in
other smoothies). Chill a large mixing
bowl 10 minutes before whipping.
Place cream in chilled mixing bowl.
Beat with a mixer until it reaches
whipped cream consistency.

THIS IS HOW WE DO IT:

Drizzle a little of the toffee sauce
around a glass. Add smoothie, leaving
an inch space at the top. Top smoothie
with whipped coconut cream topping,
extra banana pieces and another
drizzle of toffee sauce.

NUTRITIONAL COUNT PER SERVE

60.8g total fat (27g saturated fat);
117g carbohydrate; 16.5g protein;
17.5g fibre

Salted Caramel Protein Shake Post Workout

Now you can have your
salted caramel and
drink it too!

You will need:

2 cups (500ml) almond mylk
1½ (300g) medium bananas
2 tablespoons cashew spread
(or small handful of raw cashews)
1 scoop natural whey or
  pea protein powder (optional)
4 pitted medjool dates
2 teaspoons honey
½ teaspoon Himalayan
  rock salt
2 cups ice
2 tablespoons honey, extra
2 tablespoons crushed ice, extra
1 tablespoon cacao nibs

This is how we do it:

Combine all ingredients except
extra honey and extra ice in a
blender. Drizzle the extra honey
around each glass. Add smoothie,
top with extra ice and cacao
nibs to serve.

NUTRITIONAL COUNT
PER SERVE
42g total fat
(3.8g saturated fat);
79.7g carbohydrate;
30.7g protein;
9g fibre

CHOOSE YOUR NEVER NEVER NEVER NEVER GIVE UP AFFIRMATION

TODAY I WILL...
MOVE to be fitter than I was yesterday

TODAY I WILL...
MOVE to feel confident in my own skin

TODAY I WILL...
MOVE to CHALLENGE myself and make myself proud

TODAY I WILL...
MOVE to release endorphins and be a nicer person

TODAY I WILL...
MOVE to gain clarity because the clearer I am the more creative I become

TODAY I WILL...
MOVE so I can have my (raw) cake and eat it too

TODAY I WILL...
MOVE not because I have to, but because I want to

TODAY I WILL...
MOVE because it's an excuse to catch up with my bestie

TODAY I WILL...
MOVE to let every cell in my body know that I'm alive

PARTY TIME

We believe that every day is worthy of celebration, and we're not just talking about those massive milestones like birthdays and graduations!

We're forever inspired by cute and quirky concepts that we can bring to life at our next get together, so we've compiled a few of our favourite ways to party, from nourishing nibbles to guidelines that will help you be the most gracious guest.

Life's a party after all, and we fully intend to treat it that way. And when you do it MNB style, you'll see just how easy it is to sneak Active Living into all areas of your life... even the social ones.

HOW TO
BE THE PERFECT PARTY GUEST

1 RESPOND SÍI VOUS PLAIT'

2 WEAR SOMETHING THAT MAKES YOU FEEL SPARKLY

3 BRING A GIFT OR LIP-SMACKING CULINARY OFFERING YUM

4* PAY THE HOST A COMPLIMENT

5 LEAVE YOUR PHONE IN YOUR BAG YOU CAN 'GRAM LATER

6 DON'T FORGET YOUR "PLEASE" & "THANK YOU'S"

7 OFFER TO LEND A HAND IN THE KITCHEN

8 "BE A CONVERSATIONIST"

9 INTRODUCE YOURSELF TO SOMEONE YOU DON'T KNOW

10 SMILE MORE THAN YOU THINK YOU SHOULD

11 DON'T OUTSTAY YOUR WELCOME

12 POST A CUTE handwritten THANK-YOU NOTE

IT'S TIME TO PARTY

So you want to throw the social soiree of the season but you're not quite sure where to start? Follow these six simple steps that will get you party planning like a pro!

1. WHAT'S THE OCCASION?

Whether it's a birthday, a seasonal holiday or a 'just because you feel like it', figure out the purpose of your social soiree so you can plan, prep and party accordingly.

2. PICK A THEME

This will be the foundation for all of the impending fun and frivolity! Once you have a clear theme established you can coordinate everything from your decorations to your invitations and wow your guests with your impeccable attention to detail.

3. CURATE A GUEST LIST

Grab a pen, a piece of paper and get to writing a list of all the beautiful souls in your life that you would love to extend an invitation to.

4. DEVISE A MENU

It probably doesn't come as much of a surprise that this is our favourite thing about party planning! Do your research and look at fun ways you can turn some of those not-so-healthy party favourites into MNB masterpieces! Your guests won't even know they're being healthy.

5. GET CRAFTY

DIY'ing is one of our favourite pastimes, and what better excuse than a get-together to organise a crafternoon? Everything from your napkins right through to your decorations can be completely custom-made... because beauty is all about the detail!

6. HAVE FUN

MNB girls work hard and play hard – so sit back, relax and take in every moment of the perfect party you put together!

Remember, parties are the perfect opportunity to dazzle and inspire your guests of honour with your magic MNB hostess abilities.

BLUEBERRY MAPLE + LAVENDER SWILL

SERVES 2
TALL TUMBLER GLASSES

YOU WILL NEED:

3-4 lime wedges
10 mint leaves
1 ½ tablespoons good quality
   maple syrup
¼ cup organic blueberry juice
   (no added sugar)
sparkling mineral water
   600ml (20oz)
1 cup ice
1-3 sprigs fresh lavender
2 tablespoons frozen blueberries

THIS IS HOW WE DO IT:

Gently muddle lime wedges
into a large mixing glass.
Add the maple syrup and blueberry
juice. Clap the mint leaves into your
hands (to release the aromas) and
add to mixing glass. Shake or stir
all ingredients well with ice. Pour all
ingredients into the tall tumbler
glasses. Top with sparkling mineral
water. Garnish with sprigs of lavender,
mint leaves and (optional)
frozen blueberries.

Mixology

We love getting creative in the kitchen, especially when it comes to experimenting with fresh and fruity combinations. Keep your guests happy and hydrated at your next social soiree by serving up one of these mouth-watering mocktails. They will satisfy even the most sophisticated palates in your health-conscious clan!

WATERMELON BREEZE

SERVES 2
MARTINI GLASS

YOU WILL NEED:

60ml (2oz) freshly
  squeezed lime juice
1 sprig mint, leaves removed
3 cups cubed chilled watermelon
1 cup coconut water
2 watermelon triangles
  for garnish

THIS IS HOW WE DO IT:

Combine all ingredients
into blender. Blend until smooth.
Pour into martini glass and
garnish with watermelon triangle.

LIME + GINGER APERITIF

SERVES 2
MASON JAR

YOU WILL NEED:

3-4 lime wedges
1 teaspoon of freshly
  grated ginger
10 drops stevia liquid
sparkling mineral water
  600ml (20oz)
1 cup ice
1 slice lime, for garnish

THIS IS HOW WE DO IT:

Gently muddle lime wedges into
a large mixing glass. Add ginger
and stevia liquid. Shake or stir all
ingredients well with ice. Pour
all ingredients into mason jars.
Top with sparkling mineral water.
Garnish with lime wheel.

THE ART OF BUILDING
THE ULTIMATE TAPAS BOARD

We get a kick out of curating the ultimate crostini station / tapas plate / charcuterie board.

It lets our creativity run wild, and if we're to be honest it gives us the opportunity to show off our MNB skills to our party guests. Because in our eyes, ANYTHING, can be healthified!

When crafting the perfect tapas board, there are a few things you oughta know!

1
START WITH THE BASE
Find a long, wooden chopping board or serving platter to be used as the centrepiece of your creation.

2
EXPERIMENT WITH SHAPE
Collate a collection of ramekins, bowls and jars that can be used as the vessels for your recipes. Experimenting with various shapes and sizes will add versatility and visual interest to the board.

3
PICK YOUR PRODUCE
Sweet or savoury, hot or cold. It's up to you. We like to pick a bounty of flavours that compliment each other, and look visually amazing on the board. Think goat's cheese and apple, or the classic combo of strawberries and chocolate.

4
COLOURFY
It is our belief that the food should be the star of the show. Picking produce that is colourful and vibrant will make your board stand out and make it too irresistible for your party guests to deny.

5
ASSEMBLE
This is where it gets fun. Positioning is key. When assembling your food think about shapes, variations and volume. Try and strike the perfect balance. You don't want to have too much dip and not enough crackers.

6
FINESSE
Style your MNB heart out to ensure that everything is to your liking and has ticked the previous criteria. Once you have buffed, polished and shined, you can present your culinary creation to your party guests. Voila!

MEDITERRANEAN
FRITTATA

SMOKY BEET DIP

GREEN SAUERKRAUT

SMOKY BEET DIP. SERVES 4.
PREP + COOK TIME: 65 MINUTES

You will need:

3 small (300g) fresh beetroots, leaves trimmed
1 can (400g) chickpeas, rinsed and drained
Juice of 1 lemon
2 tablespoons tahini
2 cloves garlic, pressed or minced
1 teaspoon sea salt
½ teaspoon smoked paprika
1 tablespoon olive oil

Garnish:
¼ cup (35g) shelled pistachios, coarsely chopped
2 tablespoons chopped dill
feta, for serving

This is how we do it:

Preheat oven to 180°C/350°F. Rinse the beetroots. Pierce a few times with a fork, place in a small, greased baking dish, and cover with aluminum foil.

Roast until tender, about 45 to 60 minutes. Set aside to cool. When the beets are cool enough to handle, peel (wear gloves to prevent fingers staining) and dice.

In a food processor add the beets, chickpeas, lemon juice, tahini, pressed garlic, sea salt, olive oil and paprika. Puree until a smooth (or chunky, if preferred). Garnish with pistachios, dill and feta.

NUTRITIONAL COUNT PER SERVE
16.4g total fat (2g saturated fat); 16.3g carbohydrate; 9g protein; 8.2g fibre

---

MEDITERRANEAN FRITTATA. SERVES 4.
PREP + COOK TIME: 35 MINUTES

You will need:

Butter, to grease
½ bunch silver beet leaves, thinly sliced
100g (3.5oz) kalamata olives, pitted and sliced
1 medium zucchini, washed and thinly sliced
¼ cup olive oil
1 medium eggplant (300g), thinly sliced
9 free-range eggs
1 small (100g) red onion
3 basil stems, leaves removed and chopped
50g (1.5oz) goat's cheese
pinch of salt
cracked black pepper to taste

This is how we do it:

Preheat oven to 180°C/350°F. Mix all ingredients together in a bowl, ensuring the eggs have been thoroughly whisked.

Grease a baking dish with butter and line with baking paper. Pour in the mix and bake for around 25 minutes.

Check frittata after 15 minutes. If the top starts to brown considerably but is still uncooked in the middle, cover with foil and continue baking until the middle is cooked (test by inserting a skewer and if it comes out clean it is ready).

Allow to cool 10 minutes and slide into a cooling rack.

NUTRITIONAL COUNT PER SERVE
32.2g total fat (8.2g saturated fat); 4.3g carbohydrate; 19.4g protein; 3.7g fibre

GREEN SAUERKRAUT

SERVES 4.

PREP TIME: 15 MINUTES

FERMENTATION TIME:

3-4 DAYS

You will need:

600g (½ a head) green cabbage
2 kale stalks, leaves removed and
massaged
1 medium green apple (150g),
   grated
1 teaspoon of spirulina
salt and pepper

"THE BEST THINGS IN LIFE ARE MEANT TO BE SHARED"

This is how we do it:

Wash and drain the cabbage well. Cut off and save one of the nicer looking outer leaves and put it to one side. Finely slice cabbage, kale and apple.

Add to a large mixing bowl, along with the spirulina, salt and pepper. Using your hands massage the salt into the cabbage by grabbing handfuls of the cabbage and squeezing it like a large sponge. Then let go and drop the cabbage back into the bowl. Grab another handful and do the same. Repeat this until the cabbage starts to get soft.

Don't drain the juice off, it's the brine that will allow the cabbage to ferment without going 'off'. The volume of cabbage gets smaller as it is massaged.

Keep massaging until cabbage is quite soft and limp, almost the consistency it is after being stir-fried or steamed. Keep massaging until the volume of the cabbage is reduced by about half. Any coarse sea salt should all be dissolved.

Now pack the jar. Grab a few handfuls of cabbage and put them into the jar and add a bit of the brine, just to the top of the cabbage. Reach in with your hand or a wooden spoon and press the cabbage down into the bottom. Continue to pack the cabbage into the jar in this way, a few handfuls at a time until the top of the jar is filled.

Add more brine so that all the cabbage is under brine. This prevents bad bacteria from forming during the fermentation process. Take the outer cabbage leaf saved at the beginning and fold it up so that it will just fit inside the mouth of the jar. Use it almost like a lid to keep the sliced cabbage pressed down underneath the brine.

Put the lid on the jar, and leave it out at room temperature for about 4 days.

Take off the lid once a day to release any gasses that may build up from the fermentation process. Use a wooden spoon to press the cabbage down and release any gas bubbles that have formed.

The colour of the cabbage will change after massaging it, and it will keep changing over the next few days as it ferments. Do a taste test starting at day 3, and then daily after that. Once the sauerkraut gets to the point that you like it, put it in the fridge to slow down the fermentation process.

NUTRITIONAL COUNT PER SERVE
0.2g total fat (0.035g saturated fat); 9.2g carbohydrate;
3.5g protein; 5.5g fibre

SWEET ROASTED NUT MIX

MAKES: 1 CUP
PREP + COOK TIME:
20 MINUTES

YOU WILL NEED:

1 cup (160g) raw almond
   kernels (soaked overnight)
4 tablespoons honey
½ teaspoon cinnamon
1 tablespoon white sesame seeds
sprinkle of sea salt

THIS IS HOW WE DO IT:

Preheat oven to 250°C / 480°F. Line
a baking tray with paper and spread
almonds in a single layer. Roast for
10-15 minutes (they should
brown slightly).

Heat 1 cup of water, honey, and
cinnamon in a saucepan on the
stove top, stirring to mix well. Once
honey/water mixture is about to
simmer, add almonds directly to
saucepan.

Simmer, continuing to stir so the
almonds are evenly coated in the
honey/cinnamon mixture. Continue
to heat until the honey/water mixture
resembles a thick syrup,
about 5 minutes.

Pour almonds back onto baking tray
and spread into a single layer to cool.
Sprinkle with salt and sesame seeds.

NUTRITIONAL COUNT PER SERVE
30.6g total fat (7g saturated fat);
10.8g carbohydrate; 7.9g protein;
3.6g fibre

See DIY Chocolate on page 167

S
W
E
E
T

NOT QUITE NUTELLA

MAKES: 1 CUP
PREP + COOK TIME:
20 MINUTES

YOU WILL NEED:

1 cup (140g) hazelnuts
3 ½ tablespoons 70% dark,
   unsweetened chocolate ¼ cup
(60ml) coconut mylk
¼ cup (25g) raw cacao powder
¼ cup raw honey

THIS IS HOW WE DO IT:

Preheat oven to 150°C /300 °F
Line a baking tray with paper,
spread the hazelnuts out evenly,
and roast for 10 minutes. Remove
from oven. While hazelnuts are still
warm, rub them with a damp dish
towel or paper towel to remove
some of the skins (they have a
bitter taste).

Add hazelnuts to a blender or food
processor and blend until they
form into a nut butter (stir in
between).

Create a double boiler on the stove
by filling a saucepan 1/3 of the
way with water. Bring to the boil
and then lower to a simmer. Take
a smaller saucepan and place it
inside the larger saucepan (if the
water comes up too high from the
bottom pan, pour some out).

Add chocolate, honey and coconut
mylk to smaller saucepan and stir
constantly until chocolate melts.

Pour chocolate mixture into the
blender with the hazelnut butter
and raw cacao powder and blend
until combined. For a smoother
"nutella" continue to blend
until desired consistency is
achieved. Pour into a jar and seal
with a lid.

NUTRITIONAL COUNT PER SERVE
23.6g total fat (1.7g saturated fat);
25.5g carbohydrate; 8.5g protein;
3.8g fibre

Workouts for your next NIGHT OUT

ARMS

Add these movements into your regular workout for shapely arms in your next party dress! Adding variation to your routine is a sure-fire way to get results!

TRICEP/NARROW PUSH UP
Targeting the triceps, shoulders and chest, this move will give your upper body a lovely feminine shape. In a plank position with hands extended underneath shoulders, slowly bend elbows and lower body. Start with reps of 10 and build up to 20 - try these on your toes for extra toning!

TRICEP DIP
An oldie but a goodie! Use a chair and position your hands shoulder-width apart with legs out in front of you, parallel to the floor. Slowly lower your body until your elbows are at 45 degrees. Try five sets of 20 dips at the end of your workout! Enjoy the burn and see a streamlined shape through your triceps.

BICEP CURL TO SHOULDER PRESS
Using light/medium dumbbells (or a water bottle!) in each hand, curl up to target the bicep, and press up and over the head to work shoulders.

LEGS

Toned legs are the best accessory you can own and these moves will ensure you'll be ready to rock those flirty hemlines.

GLUTE BRIDGE
This anywhere anytime move is the perfect body weight exercise to target your glutes and hamstrings. With your back flat on the floor, knees bent and hands by your side push the weight through the heels and lift your hips off the floor. Add five sets of 20 reps at the end of your workout – make sure you SQUEEZE at the top!

SQUATS
Perfect for a perky peach and toned legs – try one set of 20 reps feet wide (sumo stance), one set feet at shoulder width, and one set feet narrow.

STANDING CALF RAISES
Your favourite pair of heels look that little bit better with toned calves! Stand on the edge of a step on the balls of your feet and let heels hang over. Rise up and then down. Rep out three sets of 20!

BACK

Backless dress? No stress! These exercises will help sculpt a strong beautiful back by targeting the back and shoulders.

RESISTANCE BAND ROWS
Find a fixed object to wrap your band around such as a doorknob, pole or tree. Stand back and create tension on the band. Standing tall, pull the band towards you like you're rowing a boat.

Complete 20 rows with nice wide elbows! Rest, and then try 20 reps with your elbows brushing your midsection.

SINGLE ARM ROWS
Repeat your band rows as above, one arm at a time!

RESISTANCE BAND SIDE RAISES
Placing your band underneath your feet (wide stance), tone the shoulders and back by raising your arms to a 45-degree angle.

PERFECT

BALANCE

Each generation has its own definition of what it means to be healthy. For many of our parents and grandparents, being healthy simply meant not being sick. But in the modern world it's clear that there's a great deal more to health and wellness than first meets the eye, and it's how we decipher the mixed messages constantly sweeping the media that matters.

As consumers, we are constantly bombarded with a steady barrage of the latest non-fat food supplements, low-carb alternatives, exercise gadgets and weight-loss shortcuts, claiming to improve our health and I guess, make us feel better about ourselves. In addition there is now a pill for every symptom imaginable and a drug to put every illness out of our mind.

WHAT IT MEANS TO BE
HEALTHY

But as any of us that have explored it with any depth know, having below 15 percent body fat doesn't guarantee that we will have a healthy self-image or self-esteem, and eating organic food or running eight kilometers a day doesn't mean that we will have healthy minds and successful relationships.

Health and wellness is about balance, but I believe its definition is different for each individual. It's about meeting the needs of your body, both physically and emotionally. Striving to improve your life through better eating, regular exercise, managing stress, finding time for friends and family and discovering the discipline to balance work and play.

YOGA
For overall Wellness

Yoga isn't just about working out; it's about creating a healthy body from your head and your mind, right down to your toes. The simple practice of yoga allows you to still exist in a world of chaos, whilst finding tranquility and peace through its focused practice. The wonderful thing about yoga is that it provides instant gratification, lasting transformation and the ability to change your physical and mental capacity quickly.

Try these seven quick poses to prepare your mind and body for long-term health!

no. 1
Shoulder Stand

Clarity and focus here, calms the mind.

no. 2
Extended Puppy Pose
Relax. Soften Your Shoulders, Lengthen Your Spine.

no. 3
Pigeon Pose
Gently open through hips.
Take your time.

no. 4
Seated Side Twist
Lengthen, Twist, Breath out.

no. 5
One Legged Downward Dog
Gather your thoughts.
Focus on your breath &
your strength.

no. 6
Downward Dog
Ease & flow into the
move. Awaken your
body.

no. 7
Lotus Pose
Smile. Breath. Be
Grateful. Be Present.

TWO WORDS...

Sleep Matters

IF we want to be living big, audacious lives from AM to PM, we must rest and rejuvenate our bodies for a fresh, new day.

Use these FIVE sleep hacks to get a better sleep each night, NATURALLY.

Number ONE: get 7½-9 hours sleep per night. You can't rely on your MOBILE phone to work endless hours without recharging the battery — Rejuvenate your internal energy stores to full capacity by making those sweet eight hours a priority.

Number two: foods to fight insomnia. Including foods such as walnuts, almonds, honey and chamomile tea in your diet can induce sound sleep at night.

NUMBER THREE: Digital Detox.
Technology in all its wonder is always
conveniently there when we need it, But
sometimes it can be hard to put the
iPad Down and JUST SWITCH OFF
BRIGHT Lights can stop your brain
from producing Melatonin. The
Brain's sleeping mugman; Therefore
it's easier to keep procrasti-sleeping
whilst scrolling through those
Insta feeds at Night. Ditch the
Devices out in the Living
Room and keep your
Bedroom tech Free.

NUMBER FOUR: Moving Earlier each DAY.

Get your move on in the AM
as exercise stimulates the
Body to Make cortisol, a stress
HORMONE, which can keep you
Awake at Night if it's still
circulating in High Levels.

NUMBER FIVE: Create a Sense of Calm.
Stress Busting techniques
WORK wonders to get a sound sleep.
Controlled breathing in and out for 4
seconds each is one of those few
Scientifically tested techniques that can turn
a stressed Head, cool + calm in no Time at all.

WORK
HARD

LIFE IS A BALANCING ACT

But Make Time For Fun

it's all about...

Have you ever noticed that when your balance is off, nothing in your life seems to go right? It's no coincidence… during those busy times when life seems to be running at 100-miles an hour, suddenly some of your simplest daily rituals, like taking 20 minutes to walk your dog or heading home to cook a healthy dinner for your family, somehow manage to fall down to the very bottom of your priority list… sound familiar?

Maybe it's time to begin simplifying your life. Stop over-scheduling and over-committing and begin eliminating things from your life that aren't that important. When your life is overcomplicated and overfull, there's usually little space for what truly matters, and there's definitely no room for personal growth, positive energy, creativity, love or even breathing at times.

If you ask me, life is too short to let it pass in a blur, so here are a few things you can do to escape the pressures of everyday life and hopefully create a more balanced way of living.

LANCE

1. PUT YOUR HEALTH FIRST
When life is hectic you need all the energy you can get, so eat healthy meals, drink plenty of water and make sure you're getting enough sleep. If you're feeling fit and healthy, you are in a much better position to make the right decisions about balancing your life.

2. FIND TIME TO EXERCISE
Sometimes we just need to stop, regain our thoughts and re-think our priorities so that we have time to exercise. When you're busy, maintaining your physical health couldn't be more important. Embracing exercise can give you that much needed 'me time' to alleviate the stress of everyday life and allow you to think clearer and BIGGER!

3. NURTURE RELATIONSHIPS
Make time for relationships that you care about. Don't assume that a relationship will endure no matter what! Good relationships require care and maintenance so spend quality time with those you love and feel the bounty of benefits it brings to your life.

4. MAKE TIME FOR YOURSELF
Take at least half an hour every day for yourself… don't eat lunch at your desk, instead take a walk in the park, browse in a book store, or go for a swim. It doesn't have to be elaborate or expensive, just something that you will enjoy. It's about changing the scenery of your life, refreshing your senses and doing something just for YOU.

5. LEARN TO SAY 'NO'
Focus on your priorities and be willing to say 'no' to everything else. This way you are identifying your values and aligning your life around what is truly important to you. If you try and do too much, you will be of no use to anyone. And let's face it, you won't be pleasant company either! Remember this is your life and you owe it to yourself to spend your time and energy focused on what is right for YOU.

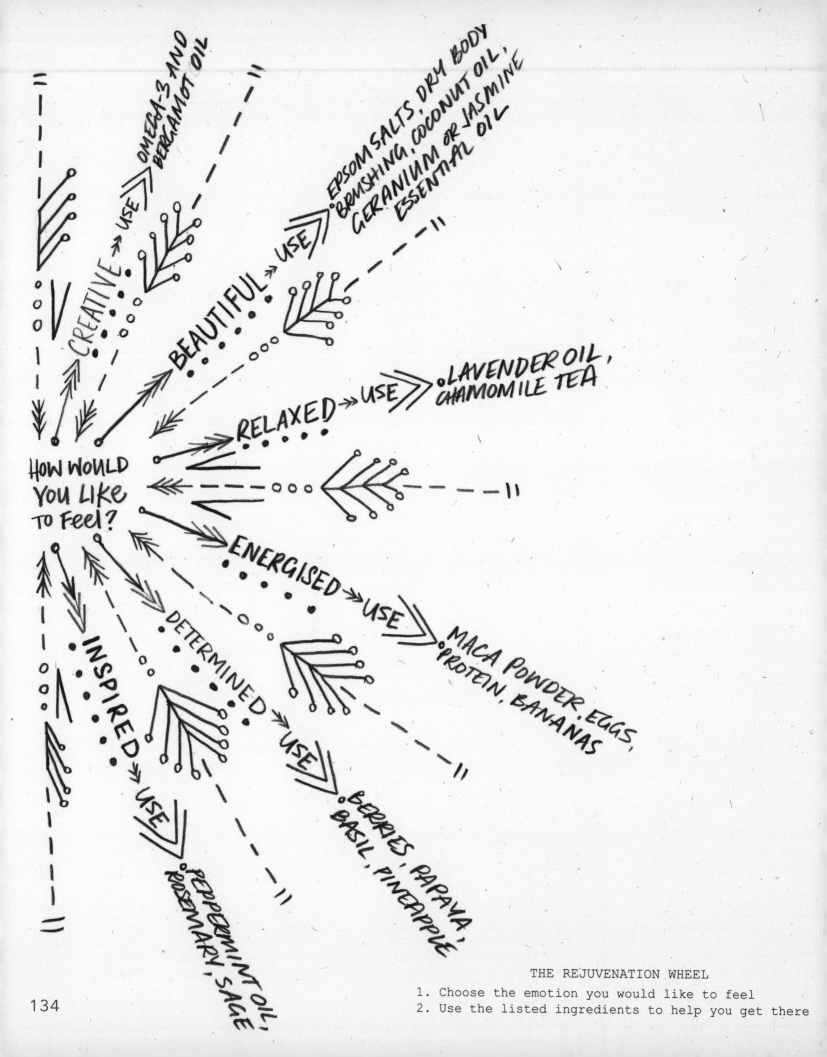

HOW WOULD YOU LIKE TO FEEL?

CREATIVE → USE → OMEGA-3 AND BERGAMOT OIL

BEAUTIFUL → USE → EPSOM SALTS, DRY BODY BRUSHING, COCONUT OIL, GERANIUM OR JASMINE ESSENTIAL OIL

RELAXED → USE → LAVENDER OIL, CHAMOMILE TEA

ENERGISED → USE → MACA POWDER, EGGS, PROTEIN, BANANAS

DETERMINED → USE → BERRIES, PAPAYA, BASIL, PINEAPPLE

INSPIRED → USE → PEPPERMINT OIL, ROSEMARY, SAGE

THE REJUVENATION WHEEL
1. Choose the emotion you would like to feel
2. Use the listed ingredients to help you get there

134

Rejuvenation Rituals

At times, our ability to feel empowered and uplifted can fade into the daily grind. While a comfort zone is a beautiful place, nothing ever grows there. Born again, new again, restoring vitality - we believe in a little thing called rejuvenation, and there's no better way to embrace inspiration from within than a little pick-me-up, a home remedy or something from the pantry that can assist on those days where you need a little more sparkle, or just to glow a little longer.

• • o • oo • • •

Creativity

Essential fatty acids such as omega-3 help our brain process and understand new information... an aspect crucial for creativity! Chow down on walnuts, coconut oil, avocados and fill your diffuser with bergamot oil - a creative favour to your senses.

Beauty

Dry body brush your body from the soles of your feet working up towards the neck. Add Epsom salts to a warm bath to relax and detox, with a few drops of essential oil. Finish your beauty bath by lathering your body in nourishing coconut oil.

>>> >>> >>> <<< <<< <<<

Relaxation

Lavender oil is full of calming properties so try dabbing a few drops on your pillow before bedtime or adding to a warm bath. Chamomile contains a number of powerful flavonoids that bind to receptors in the brain to create a calming effect on the body. Sip on freshly brewed chamomile tea to create a sense of calmness.

• • || • • o x x x • • • • || x

Energy

Maca powder is rich in vitamin B and trace minerals, both essential for maintaining energy and vitality. Add a tablespoon to your morning smoothie for an instant pick-me-up.

• • • • • • • • • • •

Determination

For a lively and healthy mind, gorgeous blueberries and sweet acai are more than just berried treasures. Berries are bursting with active chemicals called polyphenols that clean up any damaged cells that can accumulate in the brain and the body.

x >>> • o • o • • || ->><<-|| • o • o • • • >>> x

Inspiration

Popping peppermint oil in your diffuser, drinking rosemary tea or adding sage to you next meal can stimulate the brain, boost energy, creativity and learning. After all, we are constantly learning, and constantly being inspired by new information that drifts our way.

RESCUE REMEDIES

These natural, fast and effective fixes will relieve what ails you from beating the bloat to happy hormones and fighting the flu, so you can be fighting fit and healthy right round the clock.

FLU SHOT

1½ cups (375ml) orange juice
½ tsp. fresh turmeric (grated)
pinch black pepper
½ tsp. ground cloves

SERVES: 1
PREP TIME: 5 MINUTES

FIBRESHOT

1 cup coconut water (250mL)
1 tsp. chia seeds
1 tsp. psyllium husk
1 tsp. ground flaxseed
1 medjool date

GOING OUT WITH THE GIRLS

To energise you for a night on the town - sans alcohol

1 cup water
1 cup baby spinach leaves
1 whole lime, peeled
1 cup ice
2 sprigs mint
1 medium pear (230g) cored

BEAUTIFYER

½ punnet (75g) raspberries
1½ cups (375ml) coconut water
1 tsp. coconut oil
1 sprig of mint

BALANCE

1 cup coconut water (250mL)
½ banana
1 tsp. cacao powder
½ cup frozen berries
1 tsp. dry cranberries
5 almonds

THIS IS HOW WE DO IT:

BLEND FOR ONE MINUTE IN A FOOD PROCESSOR OR BLENDER

live longer

As the saying goes "you are what you repeatedly do" - and if your plan is to live a long and healthy life then you need to invest in your future health NOW!

No matter your age it's important that you plan for the future, and establish good habits that will pay you back in kind years down the road. It's all of the work you put in now that will pay off in the long run.

The good news is that you don't have to fret about the past because the changes you make today can (and will) positively affect your health and longevity RIGHT NOW.

So to feel fit and vibrant for ALL of your life here are my top tips to get you started...

1. EAT MINDFULLY

Probably the single most important factor when determining how long we live and how well we live is our own behaviour. It's about what we eat, how we work and how we play. That means eating less, more frequently, including more fresh fruit and vegetables, becoming a tea DRINKER, cutting down on your SALT in take. Replacing white rice with brown and drinking good quality water and "lots of it".

2. PRACTICE GOOD HEALTH

Healthy rituals are also important for a long and satisfying life. So it's important to engage in activities that keep your body supple, your mind clear and your spirit content. Try starting the DAY with slow stretches or yoga, take a five-minute "power" nap to refresh yourself and make time for daily walks. Breathing exercises and telling friends and family that you love them.

3. STAY IN THE GAME

It's also IMPORTANT to exercise your BRAIN on a regular basis. Having a stimulating job helps but you CAN also increase mental activity by playing "BRAIN GAMES" such as chess, bridge or doing a crossword. By playing these games you improve your brain's problem-solving capabilities. Helping to guard against degenerative diseases and increasing your chances of LONGEVITY.

YOUR BODY WANTS TO LIVE TO BE 100, all you need to do is FOLLOW A few simple rules and HELP YOUR BODY do what it does BEST... LIVE!!

10
Quick Tips For
Healing
your
Body

1. CALM YOUR MIND EVERY NIGHT.
BEFORE YOU GO TO SLEEP, IN A NOTEBOOK,
WRITE DOWN ALL YOUR WORRIES, CLOSE THE
BOOK, PUT IT AWAY AND GO TO SLEEP, REST ASSURED
KNOWING YOU HAVE PUT YOUR WORRIES TO BED TOO.

2. AVOID INFLAMMATORY FOODS
SUCH AS REFINED SUGARS,
WHITE BREAD AND TRANS FATS.

3. BE STILL. REJUEVENATE YOUR
MIND AND BODY IN THE AM OR PM
WITH SOME MINDFUL MEDITATION.

4. LOVE THE SKIN YOU'RE IN
AND GO NATURAL INCORPORATE COCONUT
OIL, ROSEWATER MIST AND DRY BODY BRUSHING
IN YOUR EVERY DAY RITUALS

5. STAY HYDRATED BY
DRINKING PLENTY OF
WATER EVERY DAY.

6. INCLUDE PROTEIN IN
EVERY MEAL TO HELP
YOUR BODY BUILD NEW
CELLS AND LEAN MUSCLE

7. EAT ANTIOXIDANTS
APLENTY. THEY WILL PROTECT AGAINST
FREE RADICAL DAMAGE AND MAKE
YOUR SKIN GLOW FROM THE INSIDE OUT.

8. ESSENTIAL FATTY ACIDS
LIKE AVACADOS, FISH AND
NUTS WILL **HEAL** AND
PROTECT ALL YOUR BODY'S
PERFECT ORGANS.

9. HAVE A GRATITUDE
ATTITUDE AND JUDGE
NOTHING THAT OCCURS.

10. GET YOUR HEART RATE UP BY MOVING YOUR BODY EVERY DAY. SWEAT, SWEAT, SWEAT

Let's Go Anywhere

TRAVEL IS ALWAYS A GOOD IDEA

THERE IS NOTHING MORE SOUL AWAKENING THAN PICKING A SPOT ON THE MAP AND PACKING YOUR BAGS.

Whether it's a spontaneous weekend away, or dusting off your passport and exploring the globe, nothing invigorates the mind, awakens the soul and rejuvenates the body more than breaking your routine.

Allow yourself to take a break and experience something new, something different.

Be inspired to see new things, meet new people, try new foods and live a life well lived.

au revoir

I ♡ N.Y.C

NOTES FROM THE WELL TRAVELLED

1. ROLLING YOUR CLOTHING IS BETTER THAN FOLDING.

2. POSTCARDS AND SELFIES ARE THE BEST KIND OF SOUVENIRS.

3. A JOURNAL IS A KEEPSAKE YOU WILL TREASURE FOR A LIFETIME DOCUMENT EVERYTHING.

4. NO MATTER WHERE YOU GO, THERE IS NO BETTER FEELING THAN COMING HOME.

5. AND REMEMBER, ONE OF THE GREAT JOYS OF TRAVELLING IS BEING ALONE BUT NEVER REALLY FEELING LONELY.

Find A Beautiful Place to Get Lost

Let go of your worries and travel light. Whether youre travelling on a whim or have booked yourself an around-the-world ticket, we've got the goods to keep you inspired to see the world.

HOW TO STAY
HEALTHY
on *Holidays*

Let's face it; there are few things in life as rewarding or inspiring as a well-earned holiday. Saying sayonara to your routine is a liberating way to pursue the things that make you feel alive, and redefine what Active Living means to you. It's time to set your handheld devices to flight mode, and learn how to feel healthier, happier and even more inspired on your next holiday.

1. DO YOUR RESEARCH

Before you reach your destination, do a little bit of research to map out the closest health food stores and hiking spots. Once you touch down, talk to the locals, or follow the yogi with the mat rolled under their arm if you have to. The choice is yours - you can either lose momentum, or let your active lifestyle flourish in your new location.

2. PACK WITH PURPOSE

Living out of a suitcase is the ultimate feeling of freedom, but preparation goes a long way when pulling off holiday style without a hitch. Keep your itinerary in mind as you pack, and choose pieces that you can mix and match easily. Don't forget to pack sunscreen, comfortable trainers and a hard-hitting workout playlist to keep you on a natural high.

3. Be kind to yourself

One of the biggest luxuries about being on holiday is having more time for yourself. Without the constraints of meeting schedules and alarms, you'll have more hours in the day to feed your soul with new experiences or slow down the pace with a journaling and goal-setting session.

4. Live in the moment

Free WiFi isn't an excuse to switch off from your new surroundings. Don't be tempted to mindlessly scroll through updates or compulsively check your emails without really engaging in the here and now. Take this time to be mindful and completely present in every moment.

5. Get Inspired

When it comes to wellness, switching things up often provides the best results, so consider your holiday an opportunity to immerse yourself in the culture and learn new ways of life. With the right attitude, inspiration will follow you everywhere.

Vacay Moves

No matter where you are in the world, we believe getting active on holiday is absolutely possible, and to get you started we've put together our go-to vacay moves that can be done anywhere, anytime - no excuses!

MOUNTAIN CLIMBERS
X 20 REPETITIONS

Start in a high plank position, shoulders down, elbows soft and not locked out. Keeping your bottom at hip level, bring the right knee in towards the chest, followed by the left knee, then continue alternating. For a challenge, quicken the pace to get your heart rate up.

ALTERNATE LUNGES
X 20 REPETITIONS

Starting with the right leg, take a big step forward and bend both knees. You're looking to create an 'L' shape with the front and back leg. Push through the front heel and step back, then switch and step forward withthe left leg.

DECLINE PUSH UP
X 20 REPETITIONS

Kneel on floor with bench or chair behind your body. Place hands on floor just wider than shoulder width and place feet on chair or bench. Lift your body into a plank position and keep arms straight. Bend elbows to a 90 degrees, then press back to starting position.

PLANK HOLD
HOLD FOR 1 MINUTE

Start in a plank position. Bend your elbows and rest them directly under your shoulders. Engage you core by drawing your belly button towards your spine, squeeze your glutes to stablise you. Hold for 1 minute - don't forget to breath!

SWITCH LUNGE KNEE UP
X 20 REPETITIONS

Start in lunge position. Perform one lunge down to floor. On the upward movement bring back knee into waist placing all weight on front foot. Place back foot back on ground at a starting lunge position. Then spring up out of lunge and switch feet bringing opposite foot in front. Repeat on other side.

TRICEP DIPS
X 20 REPETITIONS

You can do this off the side of your hotel bed or bench if you're outside. The key here is to keep your bottom right up against the bed (or bench), chest lifted up towards the ceiling, whilst making sure that as you lower your bottom down towards the floor that you are bending at the elbows and not just simply sinking into your shoulders.

The most beautiful thing in the world is of course the world itself

#ACTIVE

I haven't been everywhere... but it's on my list

We're forever inspired by our wanderlusting customers who proudly rock their Lorna Jane while exploring brand new corner of the world.

You're the ones who make us want to venture to the far reaching corners of the globe, collecting passport stamps from exotic new terrains and uncovering the newfound beauty that lies around every turn. The world holds an incredible amount of beauty and we're often the most inspired by the things we don't see or do in our everyday life. There are few feelings in life as powerful as those that arise when you fully immerse yourself in the unfamiliar and engage in the age-old traditions of a brand new culture.

When you share your active adventures with as many people as possible, whether it be through a photograph of a fiery Parisienne sunset or a tale from a trip to the Tibetan markets, you're instantly inspiring others to pack up and wander the globe as well.

So get snapping and share your adventures #ACTIVEABROAD.

ABROAD

Travelling opens eyes, warms heart, frees minds.

This heart of mine was made to travel the world

FROM AN ASPIRING TRAVELLER:

May this open letter inspire you to book that ticket and see the world.

I want to feel INSPIRED.
I want to feel a new kind of energy.
To stretch my imagination and SEE the world.
I want to be FEARLESS, break the
ROUTINE and challenge my thinking.

I want to escape the FAMILIARITY and run
in the direction of my dreams.

I want to LIVE MORE.

See new places, new cities, new continents.

I want to see life in different shades of colour.

I want to SEE IT ALL. LIVE in a new
country, immerse myself in a new culture.
I want to feel AWAKENED in a sea of NEW.

I want to meet new friends in the most unlikely
of places, taste foods I've never tasted,
SEE things I've never seen before.
I want to be TRANSFORMED.

INSPIRATION overflowing.

SPIRIT energised.

Mind invigorated.

I want to feel INSPIRED.

□□□

ROADTRIP

GREEN JUICE

TRAIL MIX

CACAO GRANOLA

Sometimes you've just gotta do things that feed your soul and nurture your spirit. That for us is a touch of travel. You don't need a plane ticket to some tropical paradise to feel inspired and enlightened. Why not take a road trip, MNB style? And by that we mean...

Music blaring our fave playlist
Sharing stories and deep belly laughs
Stopping to explore new places
Snapping selfies and making memories that will last a lifetime
And an endless supply of MNB-worthy snacks

These are the moments in life we live for!

THE ULTIMATE ROADTRIP PLAYLIST:

DREAMS *FLEETWOOD MACK*

FAST CAR *TRACY CHAPMAN*

BIG JET PLANE *ANGUS & JULIA STONE*

BROWN EYED GIRL *VAN MORRISON*

THE LENGTH OF CANADA *JACK CARTY*

TRAIL MIX

SERVES: 1
PREP TIME: 5 MINUTES

Use existing ingredients or buy small packets of each of these. Stack them in a jar in layers or mix them up. Store in fridge.

Cashews
Dried raspberries
Pistachios
Dried figs
Cacao nibs
Raw buckwheat
Pepitas
Toasted oats
Coconut flakes

GREEN JUICE

SERVES: 1
PREP TIME: 5 MINUTES

1 cup baby spinach
1 celery stalk (150g)
¼ lemon, juiced
¼ small (130g) cucumber
½ medium (65g) pear
½ medium (75g) apple
1 teaspoon green powder (SPIRULINA)

Blend all ingredients until smooth. Store in esky.

0.5g total fat (0.1g saturated fat); 22g carbohydrate; 4.3g protein; 8g fibre

CACAO GRANOLA

SERVES: 4
PREP + COOK TIME: 40 MINUTES

3 cups (270g) gluten free oats
1 cup raw buckwheat
½ cup (170g) hazelnuts, chopped
½ cup (70g) macadamia nuts, chopped
¼ cup chia seeds
1 cup (50g) coconut flakes
½ teaspoon Himalayan rock salt
½ cup (55g) rapadura sugar
½ cup (80ml) coconut oil, melted
1/3 cup (80ml) honey
1 teaspoon vanilla bean paste
½ cup (50g) cacao powder

Preheat oven to 170°C/ 350°F. Line a baking tray with baking paper. In a large bowl, combine oats, buckwheat, chopped nuts, chia seeds and rapadura. Pour over melted coconut oil, cacao, honey, vanilla and salt. Mix well.

Pour mixture evenly over the baking tray and bake for 20-30 minutes, flipping a couple of times in between to ensure the granola is able to toast evenly.

When fragrant and crunchy (to taste) remove from oven and enjoy. Store in glass jars, serve for breakfast or for a nibble mix.

78g total fat (27.4g saturated fat); 89g carbohydrate; 23g protein; 15g fibre

SAVE TONIGHT
EAGLE EYE
CHERRY

HIGH AND DRY
RADIOHEAD

IF IT MAKES YOU HAPPY
SHERYL CROW

HORSES
DARYL BRAITHWAITE

HOME
EDWARD SHARPE & THE MAGNETIC ZEROS

HIT THE ROAD JACK
RAY CHARLES

ACAI ENERGY BAR

MAKES: 18 BARS | PREP TIME: 2 HOURS INCLUDING FREEZING

BASE

1 cup (160g) almonds kernels
1 cup (150g) cashews
½ cup (25g) coconut flakes
2 tablespoons cacao powder
2 tablespoons maca powder
2 teaspoons natural peanut butter
1½ cups (280g) dates
¼ cup (60ml) almond mylk
2 tablespoons raw buckwheat

TOP

1 cup (150g) frozen raspberries
2 tablespoons acai powder
2 tablespoons maple syrup
2 tablespoons melted coconut oil
½ cup chia seeds
1 tablespoon peanut butter
½ cup (75g) cashews
1 teaspoon pure vanilla bean from a
vanilla bean pod

TOPPING SPRINKLES

1½ teaspoons bee pollen
1 tablespoon raw buckwheat
1 tablespoon chopped pistachios
1 tablespoon desiccated coconut
1 tablespoon dried goji berries
1 tablespoon chopped pepitas

THIS IS HOW WE DO IT:

Line a 20cm x 30cm slice pan with baking paper, extending paper over long sides. Blend all base ingredients, apart from almond mylk and buckwheat, in food processor until fine and crumbly. Add small amounts of almond mylk and mix until sticky. Fold in buckwheat until combined. Push base down into tin firmly and freeze while preparing top layer. Blend all topping ingredients in food processor until smooth. Spread onto the base and smooth down with a spatula. Sprinkle with toppings. Freeze to set for 2 hours. Store in esky.

NUTRITION COUNT PER SERVE 19g total fat
(4.8g saturated fat); 18.2g carbohydrate; 7g protein; 4.4g fibre

ALMOND PISTACHIO COOKIES

MAKES 18 | PREP + COOK TIME: 30 MIN + FRIDGE TIME

COOKIES

¾ cup (65g) gluten-free oats
¼ cup (20g) almond meal
½ cup (110g) rapadura sugar
1 teaspoon. baking powder
1 cup (280g) almond spread
1 free range egg
1 teaspoon vanilla bean paste

CHOCOLATE

125g cacao butter, shaved
½ cup (50g) cacao powder
2 tablespoons maple syrup
4 tablespoons finely chopped
pistachios

THIS IS HOW WE DO IT:

In a food processer, combine oats, sugar, baking powder, almond meal and almond butter together. Add in egg and vanilla and blend for one minute until it forms a dough. If dry, add a teaspoon of water.

Remove dough, form into a ball, cover with cling wrap and chill in the fridge for an hour. Preheat oven to 170°C/350°F. Line 3 baking trays with baking paper.

Roll the dough into 6 tablespoon-sized balls and flatten out on a tray, leaving room in between. Bake for 14-15 minutes. Remove from oven and allow to cool.

Melt the cacao butter in a heatproof bowl over a pot of slowly simmering water. When almost completely melted, remove from heat. Allow to cool for a few minutes and stir in the cacao powder and maple syrup. Refrigerate 20 minutes – stirring occasionally.

Dip half of each cookie in the chocolate mixture. Sprinkle chocolate side with chopped pistachios and refridgerate for 10 minutes to set.

NUTRITION COUNT PER COOKIE 10.8g total fat (0.9g saturated fat); 11g carbohydrate; 4.8g protein; 2g fibre

HAPPY

HAPPY

HAPPY

happiness is...

A lot like love, happiness is one of those things that can't be found, only felt, and what could be more magical? To us, it means always being present in the here-and-now, counting our blessings and making the most of each and every day.

Happiness is about cultivating a life full of beautiful moments and stockpiling those sweet, soulful memories that always make you smile. When you spend each day doing the things that fill your heart with light – no matter how small or insignificant they may seem – it will send a surge of joy through your core, and even if it's just for a moment, will make you feel complete. That is happiness. Nurture it, embrace it, feel it, enjoy it, share it.

Sometimes you just need to stop and take a moment to think about everything in your life that fills you with joy. When you find a way to make them part of your everyday, you're giving yourself the greatest gift of all by making happiness a priority.

Want to feel happy in an instant?
Make a happiness list.
We do it daily!

OUR HAPPINESS LIST GOES
A LITTLE LIKE THIS...

- A salty swim in the ocean
- Finding a next level smoothie recipe
- Getting lost in a good book
- Seeing your succulents & plant babies thrive
- A hard-earned Sunday sleep-in
- A warm hug from a Sister of Support
- Peanut butter
- Waking up and watching the sunrise
- Nailing a headstand in yoga
- The smell of freshly washed sheets
- Breakfast food at any time of the day
- When your favourite song starts playing on the radio
- The first bite of a nourishing meal when you're really hungry
- Laughing so hard your belly hurts

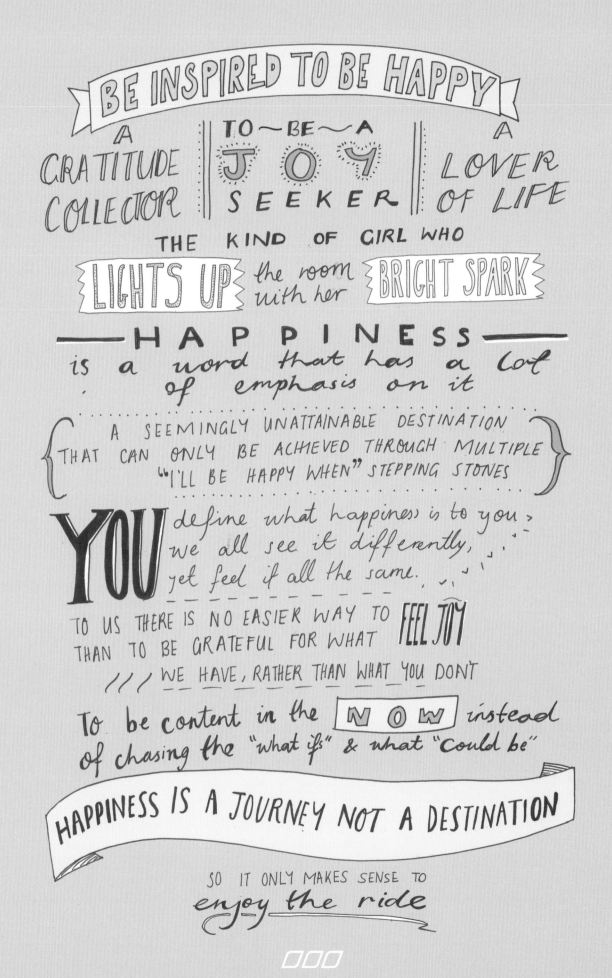

Get happy

with Lorna Jane Clarkson

"I'll be happy when I lose that extra kilo…"
"I'll be happy when my debts are paid off…"
"I'll be happy when…"
Sound familiar?

We live in a world full of endless opportunities, living lives of abundance, and yet it seems we're still not happy!

Many of us see happiness as a future state, an elusive goal, a promise of something better once we get that great job, beautiful home or perfect soul-mate. And while we often feel elated when we attain these goals, the bliss is usually short-lived and quickly followed by the desire for something else, whether it's more money, a renovated kitchen or flowers on Valentine's Day. We spend so much time waiting for this future happiness that we are missing out on the most important thing of all - being happy right NOW!

I believe happiness should be the ultimate purpose in your life and I really do think it's achievable for all of us. It's not measured by material possessions, fame or fortune, but by the way we choose to live our lives, the relationships we form with those around us and our ability to live in the moment, and find pleasure in the simple things.

What makes each of us happy is as individual as we are, but here are a few essential elements that I think can help us be happier, right now…

"DON'T WAIT FOR HAPPINESS… BE HAPPY NOW!" - LORNA JANE CLARKSON

1. LIVE A HEALTHIER LIFE

Being healthy goes hand-in-hand with being happy and although not impossible, it's difficult to be happy if you're constantly sick or feeling low on energy. For optimum health and to give your body the green light as far as happiness is concerned, you need to eat a healthy well-balanced diet, keep active and make sure you're getting enough sleep.

2. LOVE WHAT YOU DO

It's hard to be happy if you're doing things you hate, so why not organise your life in a way that lets you spend most of your time doing the things you enjoy? To spend your days in a job you love and are passionate about is one of the best things you can do in your pursuit of happiness. Alternatively, if your job isn't particularly rewarding, find a hobby or an activity you do for pure enjoyment. Think about the stuff you loved as a kid... ballet class, time spent in the library, beach volleyball and then just go out and do it.

3. TREASURE YOUR RELATIONSHIPS

Our success in life is not measured by how much money we make or by the things we possess, but by the many friends we have that love and respect us. Happy people invest time and energy into their relationships and experience the joy that they bring. When you care about others, when you reach out to others and when you give your time to help others, you make a difference. This not only brings happiness to their lives, but to yours too.

4. DO THINGS THAT MAKE YOU HAPPY

Although this sounds really obvious, many people have difficulty finding the time to do the things that they truly enjoy. So ask yourself this... what makes you happy? Sharing a sunset, unexpected kisses, pasta with friends, bedtime with your kids, dancing in the rain? Create a happiness list and make a promise to yourself to do all of the things you love and do them often. After all, it's not the big pleasures that bring happiness into your life; it's the little things that make a difference.

So when it comes down to it, happiness begins with the decision to change the way you live your life. Dare to be happy and your life will begin to change immediately. Don't wait until you've got the perfect job, perfect partner or the perfect body. Start right now with a broad smile and adopt happiness as your natural state, whatever your circumstances may be.

Take charge of your happiness. Live, love, laugh, and most importantly share life's happiness with those around you.

our recipe for

HAPPINESS

A SPRINKLE of GRATITUDE

a healthy helping of good humour

A DASH OF EASYGOING

a tablespoon of LOVE
love for yourself & for others

A TEASPOON OF SIMPLICITY

1/3 CUP OF SHARING

1 1/2 CUP OF Smiles

♥ A LITTLE BIT OF CHOCOLATE ♥

< one packet of >
ACTIVE LIVING

strawberry CHOCOLATE

CHOCOLATE, SERVES 4

PREP TIME: 15 MINUTES + STANDING

MAKES: 1½ CUPS OR 10 PIECES

YAY

You will need:

1 cup (220g) cacao butter, finely chopped
½ cup (125g) cacao powder
½ cup (90g) honey
10 medium strawberries, hulled

NUTRITIONAL COUNT PER SERVE
58.4g total fat (33.4g saturated fat);
32.3g carbohydrate; 9g protein;
0.4g fibre

This is how we do it:

Grease and line a 22cm x 9cm loaf tin with baking paper. Melt cacao butter in a heatproof bowl (or baine marie) over a pot of slowly simmering water. When almost completely melted, turn off heat. Allow to cool for a few minutes and stir in cacao powder and honey.

Pour enough chocolate mixture into loaf tin to make a 1 cm deep layer. Set in freezer for 20 minutes or until firm.

Remove tin from freezer, place strawberries, tips pointing up, side by side along tin. Gently pour remaining chocolate covering each strawberry. Refrigerate for 1 hour, score lines between each strawberry, refrigerate for a further 2 hours or until set.

Joy Bowl
with added happiness

SERVES 2
PREP + COOK TIME: 40 MINUTES

TURMERIC-TAHINI DRESSING (MAKES 200ML)

¼ cup (70g) tahini
¼ (60ml) cup water
¼ (60ml) cup lemon juice
1 tablespoon maple syrup
1½ teaspoons tamari
1½ teaspoon turmeric
¼ teaspoon ground ginger

JOY BOWL

2 small (500g) kumara (sweet potatoes),
  washed, peeled and cubed
1 tablespoon coconut oil
salt and pepper to taste
1 bunch of kale, de-stemmed, washed and
  roughly chopped
½ cup dried wakame, soaked (rehydrated)
  in water for 5 minutes
2 cups (400g) cooked white quinoa
2 x 150g salmon fillets
½ Lebanese (65g) cucumber, grated in noodles
  or finely sliced
½ medium (125g) avocado, sliced
black sesame seeds for sprinkling
sauerkraut, to serve
(See green sauerkraut recipe on page 117)

THIS IS HOW WE DO IT:

Combine dressing ingredients in small bowl and whisk.
Chill until ready to use.

Preheat oven to 220°C/425°F. Line 2 baking trays with
baking paper. Spread sweet potatoes out on the sheet,
drizzle with coconut oil and sprinkle with salt and pepper.
Toss until fully coated. Roast in the oven for 20-25
minutes or until easily pierced with a fork, flipping once
halfway through to ensure even cooking.

Fill a large shallow saucepan or medium pot with about
1 cup of water. Place a steamer basket in the pot and fill
the basket with the chopped kale. Cover the pot and turn
the heat up to high. Once the water begins to boil, or
after about 4-5 minutes, remove the kale from the basket
and combine in a bowl with the rehydrated wakame.

Cook salmon, skin-side down, for 2-3 minutes or until
crisp. Turn and cook for a further 2 minutes for medium,
or until cooked to taste.

In 2 serving bowls, divide the cooked quinoa, cucumber,
and sweet potato. Add a generous serving of the kale
and wakame mixture and top with slices of avocado and
salmon with a generous serving of sauerkraut. Drizzle
the dressing over the top (and keep it handy to add
more), then sprinkle the bowls with sesame seeds.
Serve immediately.

NUTRITIONAL COUNT PER SERVE
66.8g total fat (19g saturated fat); 95g carbohydrate;
69g protein; 17.7g fibre

IF IN
DOUBT

confetti CAKE

YOU DON'T HAVE TO WAIT FOR A SPECIAL OCCASION
TO ENJOY A PIECE OF SWEET CELEBRATION

SERVES: 12
PREP TIME: 30 MINUTES
COOK TIME: FREEZE OVERNIGHT

This recipe uses a 22cm round cake pan and can be repeated in three tiers to create the Confetti Cake (pictured left). Or create one single tier using this recipe.

If building the three tiers, for the lower tier use a 22cm round cake pan, for the middle use a 20cm round cake pan (and reduce the ingredients by a third), and for the top use a 15cm round cake pan (and reduce the ingredients by half).

BASE LAYER

1 cup (140g) hazelnuts
¼ cup (35g) unsweetened coconut flakes
½ cup (70g) seeded dates (about 7-8 dates)
¼ cup coconut oil
pinch of salt
1 teaspoon vanilla extract
1 cup (200g) raw buckwheat

Line the bottom of round springform pan with cling wrap. Blend hazelnuts and coconut flakes in a food processor until well combined. Add dates, oil, salt and vanilla extract and combine. Once the mixture is finely chopped and combined, add the buckwheat and fold in (do not blitz, keep the buckwheat whole).

Spread the crust mixture across the bottom of the pan and press it down.

NUTRITIONAL COUNT FOR THREE LAYERS
53g total fat (22.5g saturated fat);
47.7g carbohydrate; 14.3g protein; 7.6g fibre

FILLING LAYER ONE

2 cups (300g) cashews, soaked in cold water overnight
1 (200g) frozen banana
¼ cup (40g) frozen raspberries
¼ cup (40g) dried goji berries
½ cup (175g) maple syrup
1 cup (250ml) coconut cream
1½ tablespoons lemon juice
½ cup (75g) frozen raspberries
½ cup (75g) blueberries

Blitz all the ingredients, except the berries, in a food processor until smooth. Pour on top of base layer.

Gently mix together frozen raspberries, blueberries and dried goji berries. Spread on top of the first layer and set in the freezer while preparing the next layer.

FILLING LAYER TWO

2 cups (300g) cashews, soaked in cold water overnight
½ cup (175g) maple syrup
1 cup (150g) frozen blueberries, plus extra for topping
½ cup (175g) frozen raspberries
1 tablespoon passionfruit pulp, plus extra for topping
1 cup (250ml) coconut cream

Blitz all the filling ingredients in a food processor until smooth. Pour on top of fruit layer and freeze overnight. Add a sprinkle bee pollen for extra happiness.

YOU make us happy!

An instant happiness booster is receiving a letter of gratitude from our readers. Whether it is in the form of an email, comment or snail mail, your love notes make us oh, so happy.

I'm not sure there are many words in the human language that could describe how I feel about the Move Nourish Believe movement, but I suppose one word springs to mind and that's grateful.

– Sam

MNB and Lorna Jane have helped create life-long habits that have made me a better daughter, sister, friend, girlfriend and woman. Hand over heart, MNB and Lorna Jane have not only changed my life but are the reason I wake up every day choosing happiness, positivity and Active Living. That's pretty damn special.

– Gen

Move Nourish Believe inspires me to be fearless when it comes to chasing my dreams and taught me to always stay true to who I am. Lorna is my biggest inspiration and is living proof that you can do anything when you set your mind to.

– Tara

My health journey has been a long one and I really struggled trying to navigate my way through a sea of information that's out there. But all that stopped when I found Move Nourish Believe. You've taught me to believe in myself and let me know that it's okay to fall down as long as I get up again and for that I can't thank you enough!

– Nicola

The Move Nourish Believe philosophy has changed my life in so many ways, it would be impossible to detail them all. Before jumping aboard the MNB bandwagon, I was an incredibly unhealthy person. After discovering Lorna Jane and the MNB philosophy, everything changed. I became excercise obsessed, discovered fruit and vegetables and started to change my mindset. It's been a long process but I've finally found balance and feel satisfied with my lifestyle and that is all thanks to you.

– Jess

Lorna Jane & MNB are my extended health, fitness & wellness family. They provided me with daily inspiration and motivation. I could always rely on them for new and different information on how to live an active life, what foods to nourish my body with and helped me to believe in myself.

– Lia

Why does MNB make me happy? Well it's because the philosophy has been life changing (in a good way of course). I adore the inspiration and motivation Move Nourish Believe provides and the beautiful comments and love I receive from the LJ girls on Instagram.

Love and good vibes,

– Jess

I'm grateful to the MNB movement, the sisterhood, the girls at all of the Lorna Jane stores and of course Lorna Jane Clarkson herself.

I love the inspiring words of wisdom to believe in who I am and what I can achieve, the words of encouragement to move and challenge myself physically and of course the delicious and creative recipes that have made me excited to cook and nourish my body again.

Thank you for all of the work that you do and the inspiration you have given me, I am forever grateful.

With all of my love,

– Sarah

Do you want to leave us a love note? Send it our way at editorial@movenourishbelieve.com

style

IF LOVING FASHION IS A CRIME - WE PLEAD GUILTY

BE YOUR OWN BRAND

If anyone knows good style, it's our girl LJC.
From sewing leotards to building an activewear empire, this woman
knows how to make a brand iconic, and look stylish while doing it...

**I AM LORNA JANE, AN ACTIVE
WOMAN AND LOVER OF ALL THINGS
HEALTH AND FITNESS, AND GUESS WHAT - I LIVE
BY THE WORDS 'BE YOUR OWN BRAND'
EVERY SINGLE DAY.**

I started designing activewear because I couldn't find anything
in the marketplace that defined the level of style I wanted for my
workout. Since the very beginning I have always designed according to
my own personal style; creating clothing and products that I would want to
wear and have in my own active life.

Lorna Jane began 26 years ago as my own personal brand and it has grown
into a global activewear brand and way of life that I get to share with so many
inspiring women all over the world who love fashion and fitness as much as I do.

What you wear is your communication to the world about who you are and what
you stand for. When you wear Lorna Jane you are telling the world that you care
just as much about style as you do fitness and that you aspire (and work hard every
day) to live your best life through Active Living.

Our clothes, our perfume and the way we style our hair are all expressions of our
spirit and character. It makes sense that we are drawn to a look that suits our
personality, helps us express what we stand for in life and represents
something we feel.

**"YOUR BRAND IS YOUR IDENTITY AND WHAT SETS YOU
APART FROM THE REST OF THE WORLD"**

Your brand is your identity and what sets you apart from the rest
of the world. So how then, do you create your 'own' brand and
your own signature style that combines all of your favourite
labels and go-to pieces with the latest fashion, whilst
still expressing who you are and how you live
your life?

Lorna Jane x

WE BELIEVE
your look should reflect your lifestyle
and that when you wear Lorna Jane
you will be more active

WE'RE AN AUSTRALIAN BRAND,
but we want to inspire women from
all over the world

**WE CHOOSE SPORTS-LUXE
OVER HIGH FASHION** and think comfort is underated

We wear Pammy Bras with everything,
we believe tights are the new jeans and we have an
Inspirational Tank for every occasion

Even though we're influenced by fashion,
**WE KNOW THAT OUR ACTIVEWEAR NEEDS TO
WORK AS HARD AS WE DO**

We don't believe sweats are
just for the gym so we make them **FABULOUS**
enough to be worn to brunch as well

WE LOVE
intelligent fabrics,
mixing stripes with prints and bright colours
because we think predictability is, well... a touch boring

WE'RE FANS OF GREEN SMOOTHIES,
tousled hair and **WEARING ACTIVEWEAR**
even when we're not working out

We don't compare what we do with others and we value quality,
AUTHENTICITY and simply being ourselves

We cannot choose between tights and shorts and we have an equal
affection for yoga & running

WE VALUE 'WHY' we are here and
want that fit feeling in everything that we wear

And ultimately we want
**TO INSPIRE YOU TO BE ACTIVE
EVERY SINGLE DAY OF YOUR LIFE!**

Finding your signature style

The best style is authentic, natural and appears effortless. If you look
at some of the most stylish women in the world you'll find that they
are surprisingly consistent in what they wear every day. They have
a go-to 'signature look' that best describes them; an indication that
they've found something they feel confident in
and have stuck with it.

Signature style can be elusive and if you're having a little trouble
finding yours then think about those days when you walk out the
door feeling your most chic and stylish self. Those days when you
get the most compliments – those are the looks that I'm guessing
work best for you and your life. So start there and create
spin-off signature looks around them.

It's about learning what works for you, what doesn't and how to
incorporate each season's trends without compromising your
own personal style.

HERE ARE MY TIPS TO GET YOU STARTED

PICK AND CHOOSE TRENDS:

You don't need to follow every new season trend to be fashionable. Find the ones that work for your style and your personality and ditch the rest.

" Every day is a fashion show, and your world is your runway "
Coco Chanel

CHOOSE A SIGNATURE PIECE:

Think Audrey Hepburn with her cropped pants and ballet flats, Jackie O with her oversized sunglasses and Kylie Minogue with her fabulous heels. Find your signature piece, perfume or accessory and wear it and wear it and wear it.

PLAY TO YOUR STRENGTHS:

What are your best assets? You know, the things that get you the most attention. Your toned arms, defined back, long legs or beautiful eyes? Choose pieces, colours and looks that play up your assets and play down your not so fabulous bits.

HAVE CONFIDENCE:

Most importantly, wear what makes you happy so you can leave the house confident and ready to take on the world. Style is not just what you wear, it's the music you listen to, the perfume you choose and the way you hold yourself. So trust your instincts, be guided by fashion, and above all else be yourself.

"A WOMAN who owns her STYLE will always be STYLISH."

- LORNA JANE CLARKSON -

I follow my mood when it comes to dressing, and for me it's a case of genuinely feeling comfortable with myself and how I present myself to the world.

My trademark look is predictably 'ACTIVE' and whether that's relaxed-cool or sporty-chic, the most important thing for me is that my clothes have a flattering fit, look effortless and allow me to move freely.

My daytime wardrobe definitely has an emphasis on practicality and I almost never wear high heels from nine-to-five.

I favour separates in neutrals (think black, white, navy and stripes), teaming tailored pieces with my activewear.

In contrast, evenings offer an opportunity for me to experiment with new things, be a little sexier and wear killer heels that you wouldn't catch me dead in during the day!

I love a good tuxedo jacket in black or white, have a little black dress for every occasion and have been known to stitch up some of my favourite Lorna Jane shapes in luxury fabrics for that ultimate sport-luxe feel.

MY SIGNATURE STYLE

The staple items I simply cannot live without...

Things you may not know about me...

1. It may seem weird but I take exactly 35 minutes to get ready in the morning (with very few exceptions).

2. I wear a piece of Lorna Jane in every outfit because it makes my happy.

3. I almost never buy clothes online. Call me old-fashioned but I like to 'feel' the clothes and try them on.

4. I carry very little in my handbag; money, phone, lip balm, sunnies and something to snack on. But I always have a huge bag (usually my Louis Vuitton Never Full Bag) to cram my work related stuff in!

5. The things I buy and buy and buy are: sneakers, sleepwear and books!

Q&A

w/ Lorna Jane Clarkson

"CLOTHING THAT GIVES YOU INNER CONFIDENCE AUTOMATICALLY INSPIRES YOU & MAKES YOU HAPPY"

LORNA JANE CLARKSON

NAME: Lorna Jane Clarkson

WHO ARE YOUR STYLE ICONS? Anyone with great personal style who owns their look. Olivia Palermo is one of my faves and I also love Victoria Beckham.

WHAT'S YOUR ALL-TIME FAVOURITE LJ PIECE? Now that's a hard one because our styles are constantly changing and subsequently so are my faves. In saying that, the Amy full length tight will always be a favourite because it doubles as a workout pant and tights that you can easily wear on the weekend. I have four pairs so that I always have at least one pair washed and ready to go

WHAT DOES FASHION MEAN TO YOU? Fashion is a form of expression - it tells the world who you are and how you live your life.

IS THERE ANYTHING YOU'D NEVER WEAR? Culottes! Even the word makes me cringe!

WHAT'S YOUR STYLE MOTTO THAT YOU LIVE BY? Less is more.

WHAT ARE THE MUST-HAVES IN YOUR GYM BAG? Aside from my activewear, it would have to be a great pair of running shoes, water and a little bag of all the things you can forget to pack like socks, hair-ties, underwear and a sweat towel.

DO YOU HAVE ANY FASHION REGRETS? I'd have to say big hair and shoulder pads in the 80's.

A SONG THAT MEANS A LOT TO YOU IS ... You can count on me by Bruno Mars.

THE FIRST OUTFIT YOU EVER SOLD WAS ... Crochet bikinis. I used to sit on the beach and crochet them for all my friends when i was 16.

HOW WOULD YOU DESCRIBE YOUR SIGNATURE LOOK? Athletic.

WHAT DO YOU HAVE THE MOST OF IN YOUR WARDROBE? Apart from activewear, I'd have to say navy and white striped tees, and chambray shirts.

WHAT'S YOUR SIGNATURE JEWELLERY? My Rolex watch, the Chanel ring that was a birthday present from my husband and my Active Nation Day bracelet of course!

SIGNATURE SAYING... Anything is possible.

SIGNATURE DISH... Anything healthy and anything with peanut butter.

I CANNOT LEAVE HOME WITHOUT... My phone.

TOP 3 WARDROBE STAPLES ... (1) Black tights (2) Pammy bra (3) My Isabel Marant Sneakers

Lorna Jane celebrates **10 YEARS** in business

. . .

The **INSPIRATIONAL TANK** is born – with the first being Never Never Never Give UP

MOVE, NOURISH, BELIEVE.

LORNA JANE CLARKSON

Move Nourish Believe **BOOK** launches

. . .

BRW. WORKOUT QUEEN

Lorna Jane wins AMP Capital and BRW magazine's **OUTSTANDING RETAILER OF THE YEAR** of award

. . .

100TH Lorna Jane concept store opens

Lorna **STARTS** designing activewear because she wants to inspire women to be **MORE** active

The first **UNIQUELY LORNA JANE** store opens, Brisbane Australia

Lorna Jane wins **BIG** at numerous **FASHION AWARDS** for her unique activewear designs

A young **MIRANDA KERR** models in the Lorna Jane Campaign

1989

1993

1994-99

2000

2006

2011

THE LORNA

First
ACTIVE LIVING ROOM
opens
. . .

Lorna Jane is awarded the
SIR CHARLES MC GRATH AWARD for marketing excellecence by the Marketing Institute of Australia

LJ HQ USA

GOING GLOBAL -
First USA store opens in Malibu, California

'MORE'
book launches
. . .

NOURISH
THE FIT WOMAN'S COOKBOOK

Lorna Jane
HOLLAND, SWITZERLAND and **AUSTRIA**
open for business

Launch of
'NOURISH'
. . .

Lorna Jane and Bill Clarkson are awarded two of the world's
100 INTRIGUING ENTREPRENEURS
by Goldman Sachs

Lorna is cover girl for the first issue of
RENEGADE COLLECTIVE MAGAZINE
. . .

We celebrated the first **ACTIVE NATION DAY**
. . .

UNIQUELY LORNA JANE RANGE
launches
. . .

2012

2013

2014

2015

JANE TIMELINE

Like sands through the hourglass, so are the days of our lives at Lorna Jane. From sewing leotards and leading fitness classes, to building a brand that inspires women around the world, it's clear this journey has been a wild ride. This is the evolution of Lorna Jane.

where to from here?

from
Lorna Jane
Clarkson

I'm not sure what the future holds, but I do know I'll be doing everything in my power to make sure it's unpredictable, challenging and absolutely INSPIRING!

For all of us at Lorna Jane and Move Nourish Believe, it's about finding new ways to INSPIRE you. We live and breathe INSPIRATION on a day-to-day basis, we surround ourselves with inspiring things and we are driven to share it with you as soon as we possibly can.

But what does that mean for you?

If INSPIRED has shown you anything, anything at all, it's that Active Living is the key to living an INSPIRED life - a life that's exciting, colourful, happy, positive and above all, fun!

INSPIRED reminds us that life is for living and should be drenched in inspiration all of the time. But at the end of the day what happens in your life is up to you.

I guess we are who we are for a lifetime of reasons and even if we don't have the power to control where we came from, we still have the power to choose where we go from here... and that's the exciting part!

So open the door to becoming INSPIRED, take all of the lessons we have bestowed on you in this book and go forth with your best foot forward.

Remember that when you live an INSPIRED life, you inadvertently INSPIRE those around you to do the same. Try doing whatever it is that INSPIRES you and always do what makes you feel truly happy and fulfilled. Success is determined by just how determined you are to succeed, and nothing is too hard to do if your desire and INSPIRATION is strong.

YOUR INSPIRED life starts NOW!

— x

'VE THIS!

JUST when you THOUGHT it was over...

OUR INSPIRED LIFE

Behind the scenes where all the magic happens. Every day at LJ is filled with non-stop inspiration. From endless vision boarding, photoshoots and iconic events, we are 100% dedicated to inspiring you.

DESIGN

Creating great activewear is just one great thing we do. Seeking inspiration for design, now that's the fun part.

20mm wide
LP3BQ HEAT PRESS

10MM BIND WITH RUBBER

BAGGED OUT TOP PANEL

HEART BEAD

CHAIN STITCHING FOR REMOVABLE PADDING

10MM BINDING WITH 2 NEEDLE STITCH

with love ♥

elastic wa...

lace over la...

Brodenie Hem

From a sketch to the real thing, we find inspiration everywhere!

Animal print will make you run faster

APRIL 2015 - WEEK 2

APRIL 2015 - WEEK 1

studs

strappy sports bra

Appliqué and beading

fully fashioned knit

elastic waist shirred

Waterfall hemline

Printed tights

CREATIVE TIME IS NOT AN OPTION IT'S LIKE BREATHING

Each day we set aside time to sketch, draw, make and create.

MARKETING

From planning photoshoots to creating monthly campaigns, we are constantly moving and shaking to make GREAT happen!

A healthy drawer is a good drawer!

PHOTOSHOOTS

YOU'VE GOT THIS.

What would Lorna Jane Do?

Snack time! We lovvvve peanut butter... A lot

And to think this book started from this piece of paper. From little things big things grow.

the FIT MOVE MENT

A collection of Lorna's favourite campaigns to date.

LOVE NOTE
to: Nat
date: 29.9.14
note: Thank You for a FAB weekend! You are amazing at what you do xxW

ARE YOU READY FOR MORE? — FIT WOMEN'S SECRETS

Fitspiration

ACTIVE

LORNA JANE

CITRUS DREAM SOY CANDLE

DREAMER

3 dreamer candles were burnt in the making of this book.

Ash —

I've got a new idea for another book. You're going to LOVE it! Come and see me so we can get inspired!!

LX

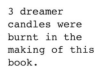

EVENTS

MNB Bracelet

A symbol of our belief in an Active future

Lorna inspires me to be a better, stronger, and happier woman. She has helped me through more than she'll ever know! ♡ you Lorna!! xoxo

ACTIVE NATION DAY!

Ahhh the magical day that is Active Nation Day — celebrated on the last Sunday of every September. Our global event encourages women to mark their commitment to Active Living and MOVE their bodies!

Some of our favourite snaps from Active Nation Day, 2014

ACTIVE NATION DAY INSPIRED ME TO MOVE MORE, KEEP ACTIVE AND IMPROVE MY FITNESS LEVEL. THANKS LORNA xox

LORNA JANE ACTIVE LIVING ROOMS

If this book didn't inspire you enough, then you'll have to visit one of our Active Living Rooms. A place where our Active Living Philosophy comes to life in the one location. Created for you to experience the daily practice of Move Nourish Believe.

MOVE STUDIO

BELIEVE

NOURISH CAFE

We love Delta!

ALL IN A DAY'S WORK

Rachel Zoe!

things that inspired girls
THINK / SAY / LOVE / DO!

Get Inspired

We see inspiration everywhere. In our friends, in music and through travel. You're most likely to find us buried in our favourite magazine, or pinning images and quotes to our Pinterest board.

Make It Happen

Other than MNB (Move Nourish Believe), there is a 3-letter acronym that plays in our minds like a broken record. MIH (Make It Happen) is a mindset we apply to almost everything in life. Impossible is nothing, just MIH!

Eat Rainbows

We believe that variety is the spice of life, so we choose colourful foods in the form of seasonal fruits, vegetables and superfoods to sprinkle, chop and blend into every meal.

Never Never Never Give Up

It's the ultimate attitude every inspired girl should get to know. We believe that every setback is an opportunity to shine brighter the next time around, which includes (but is not limited to) writing a book, working out, boys and burpees.

Ideas

We get a real kick out of brainstorm sessions and BIG ideas. No matter how big or small they may seem, stretching our imagination and reaching for the stars is just in our DNA.

We Ditch The Tech

We believe that sometimes you don't need to capture everything on a smartphone. Be more present and live in the moment... or you might miss something.

We Chant – Affirmations That Is

That internal self-script of emotional encouragement that speaks to us every morning helps us believe that anything is possible.

Couldn't Live Without Mason Jars

Those moulded glass jars make everything from our smoothies and salads to our cold pressed juices look (and taste) that much better.

Workout

We move our bodies every day – even if it's just for 20 minutes. It makes us nicer, happier and more productive people. Plus, we get our best ideas whilst working out!

Choose Positivity, Always

Because we know it outweighs negativity in every situation... even the darkest clouds have a silver lining.

Think We Can Change The World One Nourishing Note At A Time

To live your best, inspired life, you need to look after yourself. We see every meal as an opportunity to nourish, and make it a priority to inspire others to embrace healthy habits.

Aa

ACAI
Pronounced [ah-sigh-ee], these Amazonian berries come from palm trees found in Central and South America. This superfood is the perfect add on to smoothies and has a whole host of amazing health benefits including weight loss and anti-aging.

ACTIVE ABROAD
A term given to the Lorna Jane customer who is living her most abundant active life abroad. Don't forget to show us how you #activeabroad on Instagram.

AFFIRMATION
That little self-script of emotional encouragement that we chant to ourselves daily and leads us to believe that anything is possible.

AYURVEDIC
A traditional Hindu medicine that practices yoga, massage, herbal medicine and acupuncture to balance wellbeing.

Bb

BUCKWHEAT
Despite the name, it's not related to wheat and is actually a suitable substitute for people who are sensitive to grains as it contains no gluten. Buckwheat is a seed related to the rhubarb family.

BURPEE
A hard-hitting yet highly effective full-body conditioning move that we have a love/hate relationship with.

Cc

CACAO BUTTER
The pure, cold-pressed form of the cacao bean. It's traditionally used to make chocolate but it can also be used as a hydrating moisturiser.

COCONUT SUGAR
A sugar produced from the sap of cut flower buds of the coconut palm. The sap is collected and heated to evaporate the water, which is then reduced into a crystalline granulated form.

CONFETTI CAKE
A decadent and layered raw dessert, which is a wholehearted representation of celebration and is suitable for any occasion.

Dd

DREAMER
One who leads a colourful life, fights for positivity and knows how to turn their wishes into waking reality.

Ee

VITAMIN E OIL
A powerful antioxidant that works to stop free radicals from damaging the body. When used on the skin, it can reduce wrinkles, scars, wounds and keep skin glowing.

Ff

FAUXNUT
It looks like a donut, but it's actually an apple slice covered in delicious and healthy toppings. The fauxnut is fast becoming the sweet treat of the moment, knocking the donut from its number one spot.

FERMENTING
A process that breaks down foods and liquids into a bacteria rich product that yields endless benefits for a happy tummy.

Gg

GLOW
A steady radiance of brightness, shine and luminosity. A feeling and presence MNB girls strive for each and every day.

Hh

HAPPY HAPPY HAPPY
Feeling beyond grateful and optimistic about life and all of its beauty.

Jj

JOY BOWL
A delicious and perfectly balanced bowl that's made with macronutrients and oodles of gratitude. It's your one stop bowl for happiness. You are what you eat, so why not eat joyfully?

Kk

KALE
The queen of greens and one of our favourite vegetables. Perfect in nourishment bowls, smoothies or even eaten as a super food snack on its own.

Ll

THE LOTUS POSE
A cross-legged sitting position in which the feet are placed on the opposite thighs. Lotus Pose is commonly used in yoga and meditation practices.

MACROS
Also known as the macronutrients of food: protein, carbohydrate and fats. Macros are the perfect balance of nourishment to prepare your perfect plate.

MASON JAR
A moulded glass jar with a screw-top lid that makes smoothies, salads, juices, lemon water and soups taste (and look) just that little bit better.

MEDJOOL DATES
Larger than regular-sized dates and prized for their sweet taste and juicy flesh when dried. Often enjoyed on their own as a snack or a sweetener in raw desserts.

MNB INTENTION
A simple three-step formula that will serve as your daily reminder to Move Nourish Believe and prove your commitment to Active Living.

MYLK
Used to describe non-dairy versions of a traditional dairy based milk product such as coconut and nut mylks.

NUTRITIONAL YEAST
Grown on molasses, then harvested, washed and dried using heat to kill or deactivate any bacteria. It's great for vegans as it's high in vitamin B12. Nutritional yeast is not the same as brewers yeast and is gluten free.

OPTIMIST
A person who sees opportunity in every difficult situation.

PARTY (MNB STYLE)
A social soiree with our nearest and dearest where we showcase our MNB skills in the form of healthy mocktails and tapas boards.

QUINOA
Pronounced [keen-wa], this ancient grain is gluten-free and a complete protein. It's a great alternative to grains such as rice and barely.

RAPADURA
A delightful caramel tasting sugar made from dehydrated cane sugar juice. There is limited processing, which not only makes it a whole food, but also ensures vitamins and minerals are intact.

RAW HONEY
The purest form of honey, where all heating is avoided to ensure any natural vitamins, living enzymes and other nutritional elements are preserved.

SISTER OF SUPPORT
Also known as a SOS, she is always there for you at any time of day or night and has always got your back.

STEVIA LIQUID
A natural herbal sweetener to add to drinks, baking or raw treats.

TAHINI
A paste made from ground sesame seeds, which are soaked in water and crushed to separate the bran from the kernels. Tahini is a major component of hummus and babaghanoush.

TURMERIC
Part of the ginger family, turmeric is a beautiful golden plant with a powerhouse of medicinal benefits. It's also a great addition to curries, juices, teas and tonics.

VISION BOARDS
A visual representation of the life you want to manifest. Vision boards are made up of inspirational images, photographs and quotes.

WWLD
Stands for 'What Would Lorna Do' and is an acronym frequently used at Lorna Jane Headquarters.

YOU'VE GOT THIS
An anthem of encouragement Lorna Jane girls use to offer support to one another that can be used in times of trial.

ZOODLES
A gluten-free, wheat-free, raw version of noodles. Zoodles are made from zucchinis, which have been spiralled into a noodle shape with a julienne peeler or spiroolo maker.

INDEX

CONVERSION CHART

MEASURES

An Australian metric measuring cup holds approximately 250ml; one Australian metric tablespoon holds 20ml; one Australian metric teaspoon holds 5ml.

The difference between one country's measuring cups and another's is within a two or three teaspoon variance, and will not affect your cooking results. North America, New Zealand and the United Kingdom use a 15ml tablespoon

All cup and spoon measurements are level. The most accurate way of measuring dry ingredients is to weigh them. When measuring liquids, use a clear glass or plastic jug with the metric markings. The imperial measurements used in these recipes are approximate only.

Measurements for cake pans are approximate only. Using same-shaped cake pans of a similar size should not affect the outcome of your baking. We measure the inside top of the cake pan to determine sizes.

We used large eggs with an average weight of 60g.

OVEN TEMPERATURES

The oven temperatures in this book are for conventional ovens; if you have a fan-forced oven, decrease the temperature by 10-20 degrees.

	°C (Celsius)	°F (Fahrenheit)
Very slow	120	250
Slow	150	300
Moderately slow	160	325
Moderate	180	350
Moderately hot	200	400
Hot	220	425
Very hot	240	475

LENGTH MEASURES

Metric	Imperial
3mm	⅛in
6mm	¼in
1cm	½in
2cm	¾in
2.5cm	1in
5cm	2in
6cm	2½in
8cm	3in
10cm	4in
13cm	5in
15cm	6in
18cm	7in
20cm	8in
22cm	9in
25cm	10in
28cm	11in
30cm	12in (1ft)

LIQUID MEASURES

Metric	Imperial
30ml	1 fluid oz
60ml	2 fluid oz
100ml	3 fluid oz
125ml	4 fluid oz
150ml	5 fluid oz
190ml	6 fluid oz
250ml	8 fluid oz
300ml	10 fluid oz
500ml	16 fluid oz
600ml	20 fluid oz
1000ml (1 litre)	1¾pints

DRY MEASURES

Metric	Imperial
15g	½oz
30g	1oz
60g	2oz
90g	3oz
125g	4oz (¼lb)
155g	5oz
185g	6oz
220g	7oz
250g	8oz (½lb)
280g	9oz
315g	10oz
345g	11oz
375g	12oz (¾lb)
410g	13oz
440g	14oz
470g	15oz
500g	16oz (1lb)
750g	24oz (1½lb)
1kg	32oz (2lb)

ACKNOWLEDGMENTS

I'd like to say a big 'Thank You' to all of the
beautiful, inspiring souls that played a
part in putting this book together.

Sharing and chasing your dreams with like-minded,
generous people, is to me what living an inspired
life is all about! So from the bottom of my heart I say
"Thank you, Thank you, Thank you!"

———————

Author: Lorna Jane Clarkson

Creative Directors: Lorna Jane Clarkson, Ashleigh Hipwood

Creative Designers: Stephanie Antill, Natasha Saba

Guest Illustrator: Chantel Godfrey

Contributor: Phoebe Parsons

Food editors: Fiona Harrington, Ashleigh Hipwood

Food stylist: Sarah O'Brien, Ashleigh Hipwood

Food photographer: Cath Muscat

Lifestyle photographer: Jason Zambelli, David Hauserman

Photochef: Charlotte Binns-McDonald, Elizabeth Macri

———————

Printed in China.

National Library of Australia Cataloguing-in-Publication
listing has been applied for:

ISBN: 978-0-646-93696-3

© Lorna Jane 2015

Published by Lorna Jane. Printed by Bauer Media Books.

MNB LOVE ♥

INSPIRED in the making... BTS ♥

Proof reading

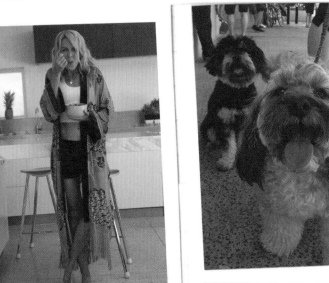

SHOOTING@BYRON

Nom Nom Nom

L + Ash ♥

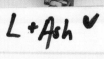

@ roger clarkson WOOF!

Lorna, where are you?

PLANNING FUN!

L + L

MORE

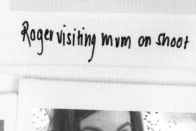

Roger visiting mum on shoot

Bill & Lorna

Stay Inspired

Active Living inspiration is just a click away...

MNB MOVENOURISHBELIEVE.COM

LORNAJANE.COM

f /LORNAJANEACTIVE

You Tube LORNAJANEACTIVE

P LORNAJANEACTIVE

t @LJCLARKSON

◎ @LORNAJANEACTIVE

◎ @LJCLARKSON